Wi...

In anticipation!
The title is inaccurate
in your household
give how well you
both cook — but
some fun recipes
for "Albus"!

Love
Richard + Helen
X

My Dog Eats Better Than Me

Recipes your dog will love

Fiona Rigg and Jacqui Melville

Hardie Grant

BOOKS

Contents

Introduction

Imagine eating the same food for every meal, every day for the whole of your life. How *boring*! Not so long ago, our dogs ate *real* food, just like us. They would hunt for prey, scavenge for leftovers and consume whole animals, including the organs and feet. With our hectic lives, we have chosen easy over healthy by feeding them commercially produced dog food, but this convenience comes at a price. Dogs are now more likely to become obese, develop allergies, experience joint inflammation, have dry, itchy skin and rotting teeth, and more. Modern lifestyle diseases have only appeared recently in our pups and feeding them commercially produced dog food is mostly to blame.

This book dispenses with the 'one bag for life' dogma and instead offers a holistic approach that truly nourishes your dog and shows that variety is king. It is easy to make these dietary changes – we'll show you how. What all of the recipes in this book have in common is that they are prepared with great love and are born from a desire to give our dogs their best shot at healthy, happy lives.

Not much of a cook? Don't worry. An unexpected benefit of cooking for your dog is that there is almost no way you can get a recipe wrong. The health benefits of making freshly prepared food for your dog make it worth the effort. Your dog will love whatever you make and think that you're a culinary whiz. We will even show you how to put together a jaw-dropping degustation spread (page 169).

Our Basics chapter gets you started in setting up your canine kitchen and transitioning your dog from their old diet to a homemade diet. We talk you through the foods to include in your dog's diet, and the ones to avoid, and compare the pros and cons of raw diets and cooked meals.

Then there's the recipes that your dog will not only love but thrive on. Our Meals chapter contains recipes for complete meals and base recipes that you can add to enhance other meals. Our Treats chapter has something to reward every pup. We even have a dedicated chapter of festive recipes because we know how important it is to be able to share special occasions with your dog.

The book would be incomplete without a chapter devoted to wellness, for pampering your dog or making special gifts for loved ones. From bath bombs to toothpaste, these products use holistic, natural ingredients, and there are never any nasties. We even consider the benefits of doing yoga with your dog.

As treasured members of our families, our dogs deserve to share the bounty and variety of foods that grace our tables. Our dogs are primed for a food (and life) upgrade – it's time to put some oomph in their diet. Let's start this journey towards health together and raise our paw and high five to the future of our dog's health. Bone appétit!

THE TRUTH ABOUT KIBBLE

Commercially produced dog food contains ingredients that are considered unfit for human consumption, which is why such a differentiation is made between human-grade and pet-grade food. Kibble, the most convenient of commercially produced dog food, has been designed to have a very long shelf life, making it economical to ship and store for extended periods on supermarket shelves. Kibble commonly contains a plethora of nasties to make it tasty and filling for your pup: artificial colouring, binders, chemicals, sugars, salt and oils. Go on, take a look at the ingredients list on that shop-bought bag of kibble. The main ingredient is often a grain because it's so much cheaper and easier to process than meat and it makes your pup feel full. Grain in large quantities is difficult for your dog to digest; dogs simply cannot convert grain into energy in the same way humans do. Kibble is also cooked at such high temperatures that many of the nutrients are destroyed. Let's face it, if we ate too much sugar, salt, empty carbohydrates and fat every day, we'd end up with diabetes and high blood pressure, and would be obese, too.

FIONA

There is a saying that having pets cracks open our hearts – this is a cookbook for open-hearted people with a desire to cook with love not just for family and friends but for our canine friends in appreciation for the affection, companionship and enhanced wellbeing they bring to us.

As a professional cook, food stylist and Cordon Bleu graduate, I have the satisfaction of having mastered many great dishes – kitchari, paella and Persian love cake – and have collaborated with culinary greats including Stephanie Alexander and Curtis Stone. But nothing has ever come close to the joy that I have experienced since I took a leap of faith and started to develop nutritious, delicious recipes for dogs. It might sound unusual that I can get so excited about liver treats for cocker spaniels rather than foie gras for humans, but I am proud to have pioneered shifts in how we care for our dogs through my company, PAWDinkum.

If we invest so much time and attention in the food we feed ourselves, why not spend some of that time improving the nutrition and tastiness of what we feed our dogs, especially considering how much love they bring to our lives? I have experienced great results firsthand – better coats, better teeth, better breath (and you know how bad that can be). I write from my own experience as a true dog lover. I subscribe to the belief that dogs teach us about unconditional love and I fully embrace the ethos that nurturing a loved pet is really an extension of nurturing ourselves.

My approach with creating homemade dog food is simple, encompassing all elements of dog health, and my wish is to encourage people to be confident and excited about creating delicious meals for happier, healthier dogs.

My dogs have always encouraged me to go further in life – to take a longer walk, to have a longer cuddle, to sit by the fire for a few more moments, to muck around with my sons … They also inspired me to turn my test kitchen into a buzzing small business, busily baking orders of chicken chia-licious treats.

The true inspirations behind PAWDinkum are the great dog loves of my life: Clover, the cocker spaniel, and Dobby, my dear rescue dog. When I lost Clover, I channelled my grief into baking dog biscuits. When 17-year-old Dobby reached his last month, I started going to yoga as a way of dealing with the imminent loss– if not once, twice a day. The benefits of this practice led me to undertake yoga teacher training in Goa, India, and to subsequently offer doga classes, fulfilling my mission to provide integrated canine care.

The other special reason for this book is Jacqui. As fellow dog people we have always swapped dog updates. The book's concept was hatched over a drink in Fitzrovia, London, during which the conversation flowed to what we were feeding our dogs and before we knew it, we were swapping and testing each other's dog recipes. As a food stylist of 30 years, I know a good recipe when I see one, like Jacqui's Handy chickpea meal base (page 82), so we joined forces to create the best possible recipe collection.

HOLLY LONG

Age: 7½

Breed: Cocker spaniel

Holly in three words:
Serious taste tester

Holly was born on Christmas Day and was intended to lead the life of a show dog but was deemed too long. She now happily spends her days in the PAWDinkum test kitchen as chief taste tester.

Favourite food: Raw meaty bones – always!

Cute quirk: Holly sticks her tongue out at you when you ask her a question. She loves to lie flat on her long back to give it a good stretch.

JACQUI

I have often said that I was raised by a pack of German shepherds. When I was a kid, we fed our dogs all sorts of food – leftovers from dinner, bones from the butcher, fish skins, vegetable scraps – pretty much anything. I loved going to the butcher to choose bones for them and took delight in watching them work their way through an entire raw chicken. I remember sneaking them the porridge I didn't want for breakfast and making them Vegemite toast when my dad wasn't looking.

When the matriarch of our pack developed arthritis, we gave her cod liver oil. A can of sardines was our dogs' convenience food. Their diets were straightforward, seasonal and always homemade. They were healthy, happy dogs who were fed real food, with minimum fuss. Back then, our dogs seemed to live forever and without many of the food intolerances or problems we see in dogs now.

By the time I had my first dog, kibble was the go-to food for pet owners. My rescue pup, Violet, was already middle-aged when I brought her home. She was a total food hoover. She would snack from my tiny veggie patch and steal dried goods from the pantry. As she got older, I fed her tinned (canned) sardines and tuna, drizzled her kibble with olive oil and roasted her pumpkin. She loved the variety; her coat was shiny and her breath fresh. What I was doing was simple and enjoyable. I fed her extra bits and pieces because I loved her and I wanted her to be healthy and happy. Making her meals was a wonderful way to strengthen our bond.

When my husband and I got Radar, our Airedale terrier, I truly felt like my family was complete. There was a perceptible shift in the way I cooked at home and meeting the nutritional needs of my family became a much larger focus for me. My interest in maintaining Radar's health and wellbeing was on par with maintaining ours. I found myself making meals for my husband and myself that Radar could eat too. Now when I slow roast pumpkin for Radar, some of it becomes a salad for our lunch. When I wilt a load of spinach for Radar's dinner, he doesn't mind if I pop some into an omelette for his humans. Come to think of it, we now survive on Radar's leftovers!

If you ask my husband, he'd say that I am obsessed with all things food (I also work as a food photographer). I'm a feeder. If I love you, or even if I like you a little bit, I'm probably going to force some experimental kimchi on you.

If you're a guest in our house, I'm definitely feeding you something delicious. It's not exactly surprising that my determination to show my love through food has extended to making meals for the hairiest member of our pack.

For as long as I can remember, food has been the most natural way for me to communicate my love, but, more than that, I use my food skills to ensure that my family will live healthy, long lives together. To have the opportunity now to encourage you to do the same with this book is pretty wonderful.

RADAR

Age: 3½

Breed: Airedale terrier

Radar in three words: Enthusiastic, confident, fun-loving

Radar is named after Corporal Walter Eugene 'Radar' O'Reilly from the TV show M*A*S*H. Like his namesake, our Radar has ESP – and incredible hearing. He also loves his squeaky koala.

Favourite food: Cheese – all the cheeses

Cute quirk: Radar is obsessed with bubbles. Trying to have a relaxing bubble bath is nearly impossible. He's busy air-biting, licking and squealing, and then there's the high-pitched barking, all to get to those bubbles.

BETTY *from* PORT MACQUARIE

Basics

We're talking about feeding your pup *real* food – the food that you feed yourself. Just like us, dogs like variety in flavours and textures.

A great start to the journey for better dog health can be as simple as mixing what you are already giving your dog with a few of the recipes in this book. If you are new to making homemade meals for your dog, you may like to start by trying out some of the cooked recipes, which are tasty and highly nutritious. Many of them can be given as raw meals too.

The thought of preparing meals for your dog can seem a little overwhelming at the beginning, but you may be surprised at how many things you already have in your pantry or fridge that your dog can eat and benefit from. Over time it will become easier and you will see how well your dog is doing on a homemade diet, one that gives you complete control over exactly what is in each meal.

Moving from old to new

Introduce the new diet slowly. Any sudden change in your dog's diet can upset their digestive system. Transition your dog's diet over four weeks by adding 25 per cent more of the new diet each week.

Week one	25% new diet; 75% old diet
Week two	50% new diet; 50% old diet
Week three	75% new diet; 25% old diet
Week four	100% new diet

The aim is to achieve a balanced diet within a given period of time; it is not necessary to get balance in every single meal – instead, look at the overall week for complete balance. If you give your pup a meal with a higher vegetable or fruit content for breakfast, just make sure their dinner is meatier.

You can add years to your dog's life by changing to a diet of homemade raw or cooked meals. Even switching just one to three meals a week to homemade food will have a beneficial impact on your dog's health and improve their physical and emotional wellbeing.

TIPS FOR CHANGING YOUR DOG'S DIET

- Plan a weekly or monthly menu to ensure a variety of proteins and meal combinations. Give your dog different textures and flavours: raw/cooked/freeze-dried/dehydrated/lightly cooked/seared/puréed.
- Keep a food diary for four weeks and keep an eye on your dog's stools (see page 18).
- Introduce one type of protein to your dog's diet at a time.
- If you cook in quantity for freezing, you will need to do some preparation – just an hour or two – to make up the meals, portion and label them before putting them in the freezer.

POO! AND WHY IT MATTERS

We get it. No one wants to talk about poo, but paying attention to your dog's poo will tell you a lot about their health. The goal is for your pup to have stools that are firm, but not hard, and a rich brownish colour. A dog that is eating a healthy, balanced diet will have smaller stools that don't smell so hideous. Dogs on a raw diet will have poo that is firm and chalky in colour with little odour. If the smell of their poo does leave you gagging, then your pup might have too much fibre in their diet.

Black, tarry stools can mean your dog is bleeding high in their digestive tract. Poo streaked with red can mean they are bleeding in their lower digestive tract. Grey, yellowish poo can mean your dog is having problems with their pancreas, liver or gallbladder. All dogs have upset stomachs now and then, but if your dog is producing unusual stools for more than a few days, please get in touch with your vet.

When switching over to a homemade diet it is normal for your dog to experience some runny or loose stools, especially if bone is deficient in their diet. You might notice some shiny mucus on your dog's poo during the detox process when switching to a raw or freshly prepared diet. Mucus is made by the intestines to keep the lining of the colon lubricated. The mucus helps prevent constipation. Small amounts of mucus are good; large amounts might point to inflammation.

If your dog has diarrhoea, fast your dog for 12 hours. Give them extra water or Bone broth (see page 81) and feed them single-protein meals like cooked chicken for a couple of meals or the Duck with tapioca pearls and papaya recipe (page 114). Adding some cooked mashed pumpkin can aid in settling tummy upsets. Also, some rolled oats in your dog's meal can act as a stool-firming vehicle to prevent anal gland blockage. You can add digestive support, such as slippery elm or marshmallow, to your dog's meals. The dosage for slippery elm is ½ teaspoon per meal per 10 kilograms (22 lb) of body weight twice a day. Adding a probiotic can also help. Please see your vet if your dog has had diarrhoea for more than a few days.

If your dog is constipated, make sure your dog is hydrated and that they have access to fresh water. Try adding extra water to their meals. Other helpful additions to meals include apple-cider vinegar (1 teaspoon per 250 grams/ 9 oz of food), sunflower oil (1 teaspoon per 500 grams/1 lb 2 oz of food) and probiotics, such as Water kefir (page 126, at 50 millilitres/1¾ fl oz per 500 grams/1 lb 2 oz of food). Impressively, pumpkin is a great dietary fix for both diarrhoea and constipation. It is high in both fibre and moisture and many dogs love its taste. You can also try feeding your dog ginger, wheat bran and powdered psyllium seeds (½ teaspoon per 250 grams/9 oz of food), which might help get things moving. Prunes and ripe pears are great options too.

SETTING UP YOUR KITCHEN

HOUSEKEEPING RULES

1. Good hygiene is vital.

- Always wash your hands before you start prepping food.
- Remove any jewellery when prepping, bulk cooking or cutting raw meat.
- Wear disposable gloves to protect your hands when preparing raw food.
- Wash all utensils thoroughly in hot, soapy water, then rinse in almost-boiling, clean, running water.

2. Avoid cross-contamination.

- Use a plastic chopping board: it's easier to clean than a wooden board and more hygienic when preparing meat. Do not use the same board for your own vegetables or any other human food preparation.

  Tip: A small board is better than a large board — it fits in the sink for easier washing up.

- Have separate spoons and other utensils for your dog.

3. Use common sense when preparing your dog's meals.

- Buy the freshest, best-quality produce that your budget allows for.
- Keep all meat refrigerated, and if it doesn't look or smell right, throw it in the bin.
- Label all food items, including the ones you make, before storing in the fridge or freezer so you always know what they are and whether they're still good to eat.

  Tip: In time you'll find that when you are cooking for the family, it becomes second nature to leave a piece of pumpkin or sweet potato aside for your dog or to make a quick batch of rice or barley that can be cooled down, portioned and packed into flat freezer bags to store in the freezer for future doggie meals. When using an egg wash for crumbing and dipping food for humans, don't throw away the leftover egg wash — add it to your pup's evening meal.

EQUIPMENT

You don't need to buy bespoke appliances in order to make food for your dogs. An oven is a great substitute for a dehydrator and steaming can also be done in the microwave.

- Sharp knives
- Cleaver (to chop bones to manageable sizes for older dogs and smaller breeds)
- Kitchen scissors
- Plastic chopping boards
- Kitchen scales
- Measuring cups
- Mixing bowls
- Coffee/spice grinder
- Rolling pin
- Cookie cutters in various shapes
- Baking tray
- Oven
- Microwave
- Blender or NutriBullet
- 1500W blender, food processor with a strong motor or Thermomix (to mince bones)
- Steamer
- Slow cooker
- Pressure cooker
- Dehydrator
- Icy pole moulds (popsicle molds)
- Ice-cube tray
- BPA-free containers for fridge and freezer in various sizes
- Freezer bags (if available, choose bioplastic made from sugarcane)
- Sticky labels
- Marker pen

THE DOG SPICE BOX

FIONA: For convenience, I have a drawer in the laundry (where I feed Holly) with a couple of mixing utensils and some handy ingredients in jars:

- Ground spices: cinnamon, fennel, ginger and turmeric
- Seeds: chia, hemp, pepitas (pumpkin seeds), sesame and sunflower
- Organic virgin coconut oil
- Rolled oats
- Tinned (canned) goods: mackerel, oysters, sardines and tuna

SHOPPING FOR YOUR DOG

· Always have a list when you hit the shops.
· Become familiar with food labels and get to know what they mean.
· Save money by buying in bulk and keep an eye out for discounted ingredients. When you see expensive pantry items on sale, stock up. Check the freezer section for discounts on large pieces of meat and whole poultry.
· Shop in season and buy locally – fresh is best. We encourage you to use fresh, local or sustainably sourced produce, choose free-range eggs and buy meat you know is carefully sourced. Find a butcher you trust and, for extra safety, freeze the meat to kill off any pathogens.
· Grow your own – herbs like parsley and mint are easy to grow in pots.

Tip: You might find a whole frozen duck at 50 per cent off that you can use for some economical meals for the whole family. Make a delicious duck salad for the humans. For the dogs, blitz the frame with some vegetables and brown rice in the food processor and voilà – a quick DIY pet mince. The wings and neck can be used for another dog meal, so nothing gets wasted.

STORING MEALS

We're all about not wasting anything, so if there are leftovers, keep them for later. Just be sure to store them appropriately so that you know you're only feeding your dog good food. Your freezer will be an essential asset for storing meals, frozen both for convenience and to ensure maximum freshness.

When storing a meal, remember to pop a label on the container with the date it was prepared so that you can keep track of its freshness. Most of our recipes are generally good in the refrigerator for up to 3 days and if they're not consumed within that timeframe, pop them in the freezer for up to 3 months. Freeze meals in single portions so that they're ready to go when you need them. For example, when making the Veggie breakfast loaf (page 104), keep three portions in the fridge and freeze the balance in single portions ready to be defrosted when needed.

Tip: Freezer bags allow for more storage space in the freezer.

Choosing between raw and cooked

Many dog owners believe that a raw diet can give their dogs shinier coats, increased muscle mass, cleaner teeth, odourless breath and improved vitality. But we ask that you be mindful of the risks – eating raw is not appropriate for all dogs. Raw meat and offal can be easily contaminated with pathogenic bacteria, viruses and parasites, all of which can be harmful to both you and your pet. For example, dogs with cancer (or undergoing chemotherapy) or with immunosuppressive disease should not eat raw food. Raw diets are also high in protein and not appropriate for dogs with liver or kidney disease.

If you'd like to feed your dog a raw diet, always buy the best fresh meat you can afford. What we are really saying is don't buy anything that isn't fresh – treat any raw meat for your dog as if you were preparing it for your human family. Always freeze the meat first, then defrost it before serving; this is deemed an important process to kill any E. coli or salmonella. We have never had any problem or issue with feeding raw meat to our dogs while following these steps.

If you would prefer to feed your pregnant dog a raw diet, please do so in consultation with your vet. You will need to closely monitor, and likely supplement her diet, to ensure that her nutritional needs are fully met.

Likewise a balanced, age-appropriate raw diet that is free from bones can be suitable for your weaned puppy. Bear in mind that nutritional needs of small breed and large breed puppies vary. Specifically tailor your approach to your puppy and if in doubt, consult your vet.

Because a raw diet isn't for everyone, we have included balanced cooked meals and recommend always including a little cooked offal a few times a week.

COOKED MEALS

There is no doubt that lightly cooked food is a nutritious option for your dog. You can feed your dog cooked food exclusively, alternate between cooked and raw, or just use cooked food as a meal topper – it's up to you.

Several reasons why cooking for your dog can be a great choice:

- You might have tried raw feeding and found that your dog does not do well on a raw diet.
- Your dog might prefer cooked food.
- You might find it easier to prepare.
- The twice-daily handling of raw food might make you feel uncomfortable.
- Your busy lifestyle might make feeding your dog cooked food a more convenient option.
- Your dog might be on the older side and find that cooked food is easier to eat and the aroma more appealing.
- Your dog might find cooked food easier to digest.
- Your dog has a compromised immune system, or you or the people you live with may have a compromised immune system. The risk of illness from pathogens is greatly reduced by cooking your dog's food.
- Your dog has liver or kidney disease, which means a diet with less meat protein is preferable.
- Your dog is a puppy or is pregnant or nursing. Getting the right balance of calcium and phosphorus to promote healthy bones and support their growth is essential and is more easily achieved with a cooked diet.

Tip: Your dog's meals should only be lightly cooked to keep in the nutrients. Cooked food is great stuffed in a food toy, such as a Kong, or fed to your pup as a treat.

JACQUI: My culinary path with Radar began with me preparing cooked meals for him – it just made sense. I had always fed him vegetables, rice and leftover meat from our meals, but when I stopped eating meat myself, I had to give a lot more thought to what I was feeding him. I was making dinner for my husband and myself when I realised that with a little preparation, it was easy to adapt it for Radar. The more I researched, the more I felt that transitioning him off kibble was the way to go. While I was already giving him raw bones, cooked food for Radar's meals worked best for us then. It felt easier and more convenient than feeding him raw food.

These days preparing Radar's meals and the planning that goes into making sure they're delicious and nutritious happens more organically for me. I am more practised and more confident, so I mix it up. Giving Radar meals that are a mixture of cooked and raw food – be it from meal to meal, or in the one meal – works beautifully for us. Do what works for you and your dog – some dogs will have constitutions that are ill suited to a changeable diet.

For me, there's no compelling reason to pick one approach over the other. We have a dog who eats everything. His meals are determined by what I've got in the fridge and pantry, what was on sale at the supermarket, how much preparation I've done and how much time I have. Initially, I was concerned that my ad hoc approach would have ill effects, but truthfully, there have been none. I am a huge advocate of probiotics and gut health. Radar gets a daily probiotic, by way of either a shop-bought supplement, homemade kombucha or Water kefir (page 126). I am sure that helps keep his system in balance.

Do what works for you and your dog, and do it with confidence. Be sure to use high quality, nutrient-dense ingredients, because this will help to ensure your dog's meals are complete and balanced. Preparing wholesome, healthy meals from scratch is an excellent way to be sure you know the health benefits of everything that goes into your dog's mouth.

GOING RAW

FIONA: About 16 years ago I received a call from my mother-in-law – she was excited to tell me that she had just heard a radio interview with Jackie French where she said it's really healthy to feed your dog raw chicken necks and wings. I'm not sure whether my initial foray was about pleasing my mother-in-law or because it was super easy and convenient to prepare raw chicken (with bones) and a cup of kibble. It fitted in with my busy life. I'd buy a weekly supply from the butcher and freeze it in batches, which I would defrost for the evening meals.

It was *me* who needed to be weaned off the convenience of kibble. It started with an expensive visit to the vet to have Holly's teeth cleaned and stumbling across the amazing book *Give Your Dog a Bone* by Dr Ian Billinghurst – a culmination of things that led me to study canine nutrition and know that feeding Holly predominantly a raw diet was the choice I wanted to make. The results of changing Holly's diet to raw meaty bones, muscle meat, a little offal, fruit and vegetables and some complex carbs (in the form of brown rice, barley and quinoa) have been outstanding. Holly has a better temperament and a more relaxed demeanour, better oral health, a shinier, healthier coat and, lastly, smaller, firmer and not-so-smelly poops.

Tip: A raw diet that contains no additives, fillers or preservatives can dramatically reduce hyperactivity problems.

The first rule in preparing raw meals: ALWAYS freeze meat and bones first, then defrost before serving.

When preparing a raw meal, keep to the rule of three:

⅓ raw muscle meat

⅓ raw meaty bones

⅓ complex carbohydrates/unprocessed carbohydrates, vegetables and fruit

Good foods to include in a raw diet:

- Bananas
- Beef (muscle meat)
- Blueberries
- Carrots
- Cauliflower
- Chicken (feet, frames, wings)
- Duck (neck, wings)
- Eggs
- Herbal meal supplement (page 87)
- Kale
- Water kefir (page 126)
- Sprouted lentils (but only a few times a week)
- Offal (hearts, kidney, liver)
- Pork (ribs)
- Greek yoghurt

One thing you'll notice when your dog starts on a raw diet is that they will drink less water at first. Don't worry. They are getting so much water from their healthy homemade diet that they won't need to drink as much.

Try out these sample raw meals. Each makes one serve for a medium-sized dog. Just mix all the ingredients together with a spoon or fork and serve.

Raw meal 1

250 g (9 oz) beef cheek
2 tinned (canned) sardines
100 ml (3½ fl oz)
   Bone broth (page 81)

1 raw egg
3 chicken hearts
1 chicken neck
1 teaspoon coconut oil

50 g (1¾ oz) broccoli, finely
   minced
25 g (1 oz) dragon fruit or
   finely chopped apple

Tip: Dragon fruit is a superfood that strengthens the immune system. Low in calories and rich in vitamins and minerals, it is known to prevent cell damage and reduce inflammation. It also contains prebiotics, which help to improve the balance of good bacteria in your dog's gut.

Raw meal 2

300 g (10½ oz) beef/bison/
    kangaroo mince
3 medium-sized asparagus
    spears, sliced
8–10 blueberries

40 g (1½ oz) cauliflower
    florets
1 egg
1 tablespoon sunflower
    seeds

20 g (¾ oz/¼ cup) rolled
    oats
1 lamb kidney
1 teaspoon kelp powder

Giving your dog a balanced diet

This chart gives an overview of the food groups in your dog's diet and roughly how much of each they'll need for a balanced diet. Over the following pages, we'll go through each food group in detail and provide you with examples you can include in your dog's menu.

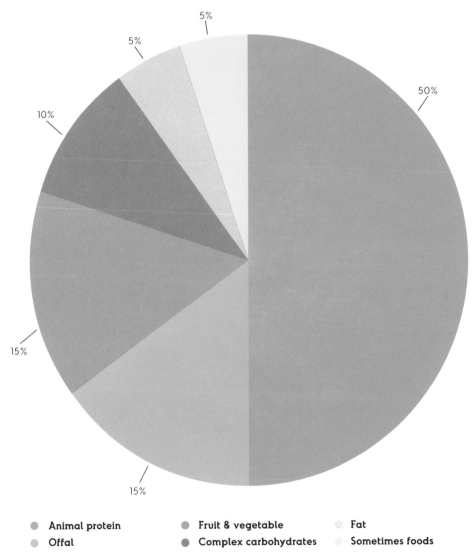

- ● Animal protein
- ● Offal
- ● Fruit & vegetable
- ● Complex carbohydrates
- ○ Fat
- ○ Sometimes foods

PROTEIN

Animal protein is vital in your dog's diet for maintaining necessary growth and should make up anywhere from 30 to 50 per cent of your dog's diet. It is a first-class source of protein and also provides fats, water and minerals.

Animal protein for your dog:

- Beef
- Fish (anchovies, barramundi, cod, mackerel, salmon, sardines, snapper, tuna)
- Game (bison, kangaroo, rabbit, venison)
- Lamb
- Pork
- Poultry (chicken, duck, turkey)
- Seafood (green-lipped mussel powder, oysters)

> *Tip: Stock up on proteins that are on special. Divvy them into individual portions and store in clean glass jars (thoroughly washed with hot, soapy water) in the freezer. Make sure to label the jars. It takes no more than 20 minutes and saves time when you make the meals.*

Meat should be the main ingredient in your dog's diet. It is essential for building bones, muscles and cartilage, and good for cardiovascular health. For example, the fat in raw chicken has an excellent balance of essential fatty acids plus fat-soluble vitamins. Fish is fantastic for dogs. It's low in fat but rich in protein and omega-3 fatty acids, which are great for healthy skin and coats. Always look for sustainably sourced fish.

> *Tip: Green-lipped mussel powder is rich in the special amino acids that are found in the fluid around your dog's joints.*

Eggs are a highly digestible and palatable source of protein that is especially great for a sick dog. They contain essential fatty acids along with vitamins A and D. When cooked, they make excellent treats and dietary supplements, and can help settle an upset stomach. Fresh eggs can be served raw, too, and ground eggshells can be used as a meal add-on. If chicken eggs are a no-go due to allergy, duck eggs are an excellent alternative.

JACQUI: I often hard-boil eggs for Radar, keep them in the fridge and feed them to him either whole as a snack (with the shell a little smashed for easier access) or sliced in his meal – the shell and all.

RAW MEATY BONES

Bones are packed full of nutrients that are vital to your dog's health. Bone meat and meaty bones contain calcium and many nutrients that build bones, promote healthy teeth and gums, and release happy hormones. They're excellent for gut health and getting rid of doggie odour. They're the natural beauty food for our dogs' inner and outer health.

Bones are also full of blood-forming nutrients (these are found in the marrow), including copper and iron. For example, the bones in raw chicken wings are full of iron-containing marrow, which can help build your dog's immune system.

Bones are great for cleaning your dog's teeth. When dogs chew and rip the flesh off bones, they massage their gums and clean their teeth. Raw meaty bones can prevent gum disease, dental cavities, tooth root decay and dental abscesses. Chewing on a large meaty bone provides great exercise for dogs and keeps them from getting bored.

Raw meaty bones, such as chicken wings and necks, are high in moisture content, softer, more flexible and very easily digested. They should be an integral part of your dog's raw diet because they contain nutrients such as glucosamine and chondroitin, essential omega fatty acids and bone-building minerals, such as calcium, phosphorus and magnesium.

Never feed your dog cooked bones. Cooked bones are low in moisture and can easily splinter and become a choking hazard or cause serious injury to your dog's digestive system. Also avoid feeding your dog weight-bearing bones. These are the leg bones of animals and include: lamb shank, turkey and chicken leg. These bones are hard, have a tendency to splinter and can crack their teeth, resulting in an expensive trip to the vet. Chicken legs should be chopped before you feed them to your dog.

Bones aren't just for large dogs. Choosing a bone that is the right size for your dog is extremely important. Small beef bones are ideal for smaller dogs, whereas larger dogs should avoid small bones, as they may pose a choking hazard. Get your pups started on raw meaty bones from an early age with chicken wings or necks. Your pups will love them and are perfectly capable of digesting them.

Tip: It's best to chop chicken or duck necks before serving; they can get lodged in your dog's throat if they're not chewing properly.

Bones for your dog:

- Beef (brisket, ribs, tail)
- Chicken (feet, frame, necks, wings)
- Duck (feet, frame, necks, wings)
- Emu (necks, ribs)
- Fish (whole sardines, salmon heads and frames)
- Goat (necks, ribs, spine)
- Kangaroo (ribs, tails)
- Lamb (necks, ribs, spine)
- Pork (brisket, necks, ribs)
- Quail (whole or pieces)
- Rabbit (whole or pieces)
- Turkey (feet, frame, necks)

WHEN FEEDING BONES TO YOUR DOG

Supervise your pet until you are confident that they can handle eating bones.

Separate your dogs if you are a multi-dog household to avoid any bone-related brawls.

Size matters. Start with a bone larger than the size of your pet's head to ensure that it can't be swallowed.

FIONA: It can be heartwarming to watch your dog chewing on a bone, releasing happy endorphins not just in them but also in you. I was a late convert because I was worried about the mess and the risk of choking. This fear actually put a big dent in my wallet. I had to fork out $1000 to have Holly's teeth cleaned – ouch! – before I stumbled on *Give Your Dog a Bone* in a second-hand bookstore. From then on, it made complete sense to me to feed my dogs raw meaty bones.

OFFAL

Offal or organ meat is an excellent source of energy for dogs who are active, growing or stressed. It contains quality protein and healthy fats, as well as essential fatty acids, which help them absorb vitamins.

Nutrients are allocated to the parts of your dog's body that need them most. Brain and joint function take priority over their skin and coat; if your dog's skin and coat are not in good condition, your dog could be lacking key nutrients.

You will be blown away by the glowing benefits of feeding your dog a little offal with their meal. We know it's a bit of an off subject, but not only do dogs love offal, it is also very good for their inner and outer health. It can help to keep their skin healthy and their coats shiny, and it helps with their reproductive health as well as promoting a good temperament.

Offal makes a highly nutritious training treat (see pages 141-142). Always give offal in small portions: it should make up about 10 per cent of an adult dog's diet. (Dogs that are reproducing can have a little more.)

Be sure to buy offal from a trusted source, or only use offal from poultry to avoid parasites and hydatid cysts. It is important to freeze all offal below −20°C for up to ten days to reduce the risk of parasites and hydatid cysts. Cooking offal will also kill any hydatid cysts.

JACQUI: Radar loves all things offal. I keep chicken hearts, fish skins, liver and beef windpipe (trachea), as well as sprats and anything else I feel a bit squeamish about, bagged and in the freezer. I feed them to Radar frozen, either as part of his meal or as a snack.

Offal for your dog:

- Brains – rich in protein, fat and water. These are not suitable for a dog with cholesterol problems.
- Chicken feet – rich in glucosamine and chondroitin, which can help your dog maintain joint health and reduce joint pain caused by age or arthritis.
- Green tripe (the untreated contents of a grazing animal's stomach or intestines) – contains plenty of enzymes, good bacteria and nutrients that are excellent for your dog's health.
- Beef/chicken hearts – excellent source of protein, B vitamins, iron and some essential fatty acids. Chicken hearts are a convenient size ,which means less mess. They also make the best little dehydrated reward/high-value training treat (see page 141).
- Kidneys – excellent source of protein, and also provide essential fatty acids and fat-soluble vitamins A, D, E and K. Kidneys contain selenium, which is necessary for the normal functioning of the immune system. Beef, lamb and pork kidney have good levels of selenium (but pork kidney has a lot more sodium). Dehydrated kidneys make another high-value training treat (see page 141).
- Beef/chicken livers – excellent source of protein, minerals (zinc, manganese, selenium and iron), essential fatty acids (omega-3 and omega-6) and vitamin A. These are not suitable for obese dogs or those with cholesterol problems. Beef liver is a rich source of copper – this helps the absorption of iron, which is important for red blood cell function.
- Pork trotters – a natural food for dogs that's great for their teeth.
- Tongue – full of protein, fat, water and vitamin B, but can be a bit fatty.

Tip: Get some little freezer containers with lids, cut up offal once a month and freeze so you always have it conveniently at hand to defrost for each meal.

COMPLEX CARBOHYDRATES

Complex carbohydrates are king: they are a slow-releasing form of energy, aid digestion, help regulate the metabolism, keep the immune system strong and support the nervous system. Complex carbs should make up no more than 10 to 15 per cent of your dog's daily diet.

Grains are one type of complex carbohydrate and are nutritious sources of protein, vitamins and minerals; in moderate, well-balanced quantities, they have not been found to cause any health problems for dogs.

<u>FIONA</u>: I like to cook large batches of brown rice, quinoa and lentils, and store them in handy-sized batches so I always have them on hand when I need. I keep what I will use within 3 days in the fridge and freeze the rest – it keeps well for 3 months.

Complex carbohydrates for your dog:

· Amaranth
· Couscous
· Freekeh
· Oats – rich in magnesium; support the nervous system.
· Pearl barley
· Pumpkin
· Psyllium
· Quinoa – contains high levels of essential amino acids. The edible seed of quinoa is full of nutrients and when cooked makes a healthy alternative to corn, wheat and soy. It's best to wash quinoa before cooking to get rid of saponin, which can cause intestinal irritation. (Saponin is produced by the plant to protect itself from insects.)
· Rice (basmati, brown)
· Sweet potato – high in dietary fibre (which helps support the digestive system), low in fat and contains essential vitamins like A, B6 and C. Sweet potato has more than double the calories of pumpkin so choose pumpkin if your dog is overweight.
· Tapioca pearls
· Wheatgerm – good source of fibre that is high in vitamins B and E, folic acid and essential fatty acids.

CANINE DILATED CARDIOMYOPATHY (DCM)

Studies are currently taking place to examine the potential link between grain-free diets and canine dilated cardiomyopathy (DCM) in dogs. DCM reduces the heart's ability to pump blood around the body and is a prevalent heart disease that affects dogs, particularly large-breed dogs. The thought is that dogs who eat certain grain-free dog foods develop DCM more commonly. Studies are ongoing and so far inconclusive. High levels of legumes, pulses or potatoes are more common in diets labelled as grain-free, but it's not yet known how these ingredients might be linked to DCM.

VEGETABLES

Vegetables are an important part of your dog's diet as a source of energy, vitamins, minerals and fibre. They should make up 15 per cent of your dog's diet. Feed your dog a rainbow of fruits and vegetables for optimum health benefits. Improve your dog's health by incorporating some green leafy vegetables and orange and yellow vegetables into their diet at least three times a week.

Dogs cannot digest large pieces of uncooked vegetables. Dogs don't chew their food like we do to pulp vegetables (their jaws only move up and down, not side to side) and they don't have the enzymes to digest the cellulose in plant cell walls. To help your dog digest and absorb the nutrients from vegetables, they should be finely chopped, lightly steamed or puréed.

In the wild, dogs would systematically eat their prey. The stomach and its contents would be one of the first parts they eat. Pulverising vegetables through a food processor or juicer mimics the contents of the prey's stomach.

Tip: Fermented vegetables are easy for your dog to digest and excellent for maintaining good gut bacteria. Add to your pup's main meal or mix into a smoothie for an instant gut health boost (see pages 129–131).

VEGETABLE	NUTRITIONAL VALUE	MEAL SUGGESTIONS
Asparagus	High in fibre and vitamins C, E and K; supports the digestive system	Raw meal 2 (page 31)
Beans (green, purple, broadbeans, edamame)	High in B vitamins (which support the nervous and cardiovascular systems), potassium, magnesium and iron	Energy porridge (page 98) Cheat's dinner (page 109) Tuna mac (page 108) Christmas cake (page 163)
Beetroot (beets) (purple, yellow, white)	A great source of fibre, folate (vitamin B9), manganese, potassium, iron and vitamin C; supports the cardiovascular system	Veggie breakfast loaf (page 104) Beetroot pesto (page 84) DIY pet mince (page 93) Red velvet pupcakes (page 158) Diwali festival cake (page 160)
Broccoli	High in fibre, calcium, potassium and vitamins C and K, and low in fat; this powerhouse veggie supports the digestive, cardiovascular and immune systems	Meatless loaf (page 103) Raw meal 1 (page 30)
Brussels sprouts (green, purple)	Rich in vitamins, including A, B1, B6 and C, a great source of fibre and full of antioxidants; supports digestive and cardiovascular systems	Duck with lentils and apple (page 115) Dog's pork roast (page 110),
Cabbage (white, purple, Tuscan)	Packed full of antioxidants and vitamin K; good for skin, heart and joint health	Add greens (page 48) Chicken and fennel meatballs (page 94) Meatless loaf (page 103)
Capsicum (bell peppers) (red, yellow)	A great source of lutein and vitamins A, B6, C and E (vitamin C and beta-carotene, are important antioxidants for the immune system); good for heart health	Middle Eastern lamb with pumpkin and barley (page 111)

VEGETABLE	NUTRITIONAL VALUE	MEAL SUGGESTIONS
Carrot (orange, yellow, purple)	High in vitamin A, fibre and potassium; boosts the immune system	Veggie breakfast loaf (page 104) Duck with lentils and apple (page 115) Chicken and fennel meatballs (page 94) Vietnamese pork meatballs (page 95) Slow-cooked brisket with Mediterranean vegetables (page 116) DIY pet mince (page 93) Bone broth (page 81) Bone broth iced treat (page 125) Christmas cake (page 163) Carrot treats (page 140)
Cauliflower	A good source of fibre, calcium, potassium, folate and vitamins C and K; good for the muscular, cardiovascular and immune systems	Raw meal 2 (page 31)
Celeriac	High in vitamins A and K; good for the digestive and cardiovascular systems	Add to any main meal
Celery	Contains fibre, folate, potassium, manganese and vitamins A, C and K, and low in fat and cholesterol; good for the cardiovascular and digestive systems	Add greens (page 48) Slow-cooked brisket with Mediterranean vegetables (page 116) Bone broth (page 81) Bone broth iced treat (page 125) Immune-boosting green smoothie (page 131)
Corn kernels	Good source of fibre, essential fatty acids, protein and antioxidants; support the digestive system	Energy porridge (page 98) Cheat's dinner (page 109) Tuna mac (page 108) Christmas cake (page 163)

VEGETABLE	NUTRITIONAL VALUE	MEAL SUGGESTIONS
Cucumber	Good source of potassium and vitamin C, and low in fat; balances hydration, lowers blood sugar levels and supports the cardiovascular system	Add greens (page 48)
Fennel	Contains calcium, iron, potassium and vitamins A and C; supports the digestive system	Slow-cooked brisket with Mediterranean vegetables (page 116)
Green leafy vegetables	High in fibre; a good source of calcium, potassium and magnesium and rich in antioxidants and vitamins; also possess cleansing and pH-balancing properties, support the cardiovascular system and have all-over health benefits	Vietnamese pork meatballs (page 95) Fishy bean pie (page 118)
Kale (green, purple)	Rich in vitamins A, C and K; supports the cardiovascular system	Meatless loaf (page 103)
Peas	Contain iron, zinc, potassium, magnesium, protein and vitamins A, B and K; support the cardiovascular and immune systems	Energy porridge (page 98) Cheat's dinner (page 109) Tuna mac (page 108) Christmas cake (page 163)
Potato	Great source of calcium, potassium, magnesium, iron and vitamins A, B6 and C; supports the digestive, cardiovascular and circulatory systems	Moroccan lamb hotpot with freekeh (page 117) Fishy bean pie (page 118) Party cake (page 157)
Pumpkin	Contains antioxidants, fibre and vitamin A; good for eye health, as well as the cardiovascular, circulatory, digestive and immune systems	Pumpkin and oat risotto (page 102) Beef and pumpkin risotto (page 100) Middle Eastern lamb with pumpkin and barley (page 111) Slow-cooked brisket with Mediterranean vegetables (page 116) Pumpkin pie biscotti (page 144)

VEGETABLE	NUTRITIONAL VALUE	MEAL SUGGESTIONS
Radish (including leaves)	Good source of fibre, potassium and vitamin C, and the antioxidant anthocyanin, which improves brain function; the leaves are high in vitamins B6 and C; supports the digestive system	Leaves: Green pesto (page 84)
Silverbeet (Swiss chard)	Contains manganese, potassium, calcium, copper, iron and vitamins A, C and K; supports the nervous and cardiovascular systems	Beef and pumpkin risotto (page 100) DIY pet mince (page 93)
Spinach	High in vitamins A, B, C and K and rich in antioxidants and beta-carotene; good for the cardiovascular system and for eye health	Veggie breakfast loaf (page 104) Beef burgers (page 97) Immune-boosting green smoothie (page 131) Green pesto (page 84) Meatless loaf (page 103)
Squash	High in fibre, low in calories, and a good source of nutrients; good for the immune system and eye health	Add to any main meal
Swede (rutabaga)	High in vitamins C, B6, E and K; supports the digestive and immune systems	Add to any main meal
Sweet potato	High in fibre and a good source of manganese and vitamins A and C; good for the digestive system and the immune system	Dog's pork roast (page 110) Beef burgers (page 97) Sweet potato wedges (page 82) Hanukkah doughnuts (page 164) Meatless loaf (page 103)
Turnip	A good source of vitamin C, calcium, folate, manganese, potassium, magnesium, iron, calcium, phosphorus, omega-3 and protein, and low in calories; support the cardiovascular system	Add to any main meal
Zucchini (courgette) (green, yellow)	High in fibre, vitamins and minerals; good for the digestive and cardiovascular systems and for eye health	Beef burgers (page 97) DIY pet mince (page 93) Banana peanut butter nice cream (page 133) Immune-boosting green smoothie (page 131)

ANTIOXIDANTS

Antioxidants help fight free radicals, which are responsible for cellular and molecular damage. They are especially beneficial for dogs with arthritis and dogs past middle age because they can slow the process of cellular degeneration that causes ageing. Food enriched with antioxidants decreases the rate of cognitive decline and improves behaviour.

Pick purple when you can. All purple fruits and vegetables contain the antioxidant anthocyanin, which works to protect your dog's brain cells and lower their risk of getting cancer. It also reduces inflammation.

Vegetables and fruit rich in antioxidants:

- Apple
- Broccoli
- Brussels sprouts
- Green capsicum (bell pepper)
- Carrot
- Kale
- Peach
- Spinach
- Squash
- Strawberries
- Tomato

ADD GREENS

FIONA: Help the planet by feeding your dog your own food scraps. Use the pulp left over after juicing to make the Veggie breakfast loaf (page 104) or mix the pulp with 60 ml (2 fl oz/¼ cup) of veggie juice to make up part of your dog's evening meal. When trimming your veggies for your own meal, keep the bits you would otherwise discard and use them in your dog's meal.

Here's a quick way to add greens to your dog's diet. Any green veggie will work – use cucumber trimmings, the fresh green tops of carrots, outer celery leaves and a few bigger cabbage leaves. Blitz to a purée in a food processor with a little water and a splash of apple-cider vinegar or a little Bone broth (page 81). Divide and store individual portions in containers to add to your dog's meals. Keep in the fridge for up to 3 days or freeze for up to 3 months.

GARLIC – YES OR NO?

We say yes. But only in safe quantities – the dosing is important to get right.

<u>JACQUI</u>: It's safe to feed your dog ¼ clove of garlic per 5 kilograms (11 lb) of their weight. Radar, who weighs 30 kilograms (66 lb), can safely consume one clove.

Garlic belongs to the genus *Allium*, as do onions, leeks and chives. When consumed in large amounts, alliums can cause gastroenteritis, abdominal pain, vomiting and diarrhoea. The deadly aspect of alliums' toxicity is their effect on red blood cells, which can rupture, and may result in anaemia, an increased heart rate, collapsed lungs and death.

However, we feel that feeding garlic in small quantities, and occasionally, is beneficial for your pup. Garlic has antifungal and antibacterial properties, helps combat fleas and boosts your dog's immune system.

It is important to keep in mind that garlic is dangerous when fed improperly and can clash with some medications. Steer clear of processed garlic powder.

LEGUMES

Legumes are highly nutritious, being packed with protein, carbohydrates, fibre, vitamins and minerals. A cup of cooked chickpeas contains almost 15 grams (½ oz) of protein; likewise a cup of cooked lentils contains just under 18 grams (a little more than ½ oz) of protein. That's a lot of plant-based protein (a 150 gram (5½ oz) steak contains 44 grams [1½ oz] of protein). Peanuts are also legumes; I've never met a dog who doesn't love a treat of peanut butter. That said, be mindful not to overdo the legumes because too much fibre can cause gas and bowel irritation.

Legumes for your dog:

· Sprouted alfalfa
· Beans (black beans, kidney beans) – can be used as icing for a dog cake (see Fudge icing, page 167).
· Lentils – high in potassium, which maintains the body's fluid and reduces puffiness. Sprouted lentils are a live food that is an excellent source of increased crude fibre and fatty acids; sprouting the lentils improves the absorption of the minerals and vitamins that lentils contain and makes them easier to digest. Sprouted lentils make a delicious meal topper.

JACQUI: I feed Radar lentils regularly and he loves them. I prefer to give him mung dal lentils; they are split, so are easy to digest and quick to cook. Chickpeas are also a good option – see my delicious Handy chickpea meal base (page 82).

PEANUT BUTTER

Peanuts are safe for dogs in small quantities, as long as they are unsalted and unseasoned. In moderation, peanut butter can be a good source of protein and healthy fat. The best and only peanut butter for dogs is one that has only peanuts in it. Make sure it *never* contains xylitol, a sweetener that is used in many food products. Although xylitol is safe for humans, it is potentially deadly for dogs and if ingested, it can cause seizures, liver failure and death.

SEEDS

Many of the same seeds we incorporate into our diet (such as linseeds [flax seeds], chia, pumpkin and sunflower) are also healthy choices for our dogs. Linseeds are jam-packed with goodness. They contain a special group of plant-based compounds called lignans, which fight inflammation and in turn help support your dog's immune system. Linseeds are a good source of protein and fibre, and will help to improve the condition of your dog's skin and fur too. Pepitas (pumpkin seeds) are rich in protein, fibre, amino acids, phosphorus, copper, iron, magnesium, potassium, niacin and zinc.

Seeds for your dog:

- Chia – full of omega-3 and antioxidants; good for brain and heart health.
- Hemp – a superfood rich in protein, fibre, antioxidants and healthy fatty acids, including omega-3 and omega-6. They are good for the brain and beneficial for the health of your dog's heart, skin and joints.
- Linseeds (flax seeds) – packed full of antioxidants; beneficial for the skin and coat. Go for ground linseeds and soak them first for easy digestion.
- Pepitas (pumpkin seeds) – good for the digestive system and a great source of omega-3, fibre, protein, iron, copper and zinc (which helps rebuild collagen and improve skin health).
- Sesame – contain healthy fats, minerals and vitamins B and E; protect the liver, combat arthritis and may also help with bone health.
- Sunflower – excellent source of vitamin E and omega-3; good for skin and heart health and a good source of energy.

Tip: Keep at hand a jar of seeds, made up of ½ cup sesame seeds, ½ cup sunflower seeds, ½ cup pepitas (pumpkin seeds) and ½ cup linseeds (flax seeds). Whiz up in a clean coffee grinder. This mixture is packed full of beneficial fats and is a concentrated source of vitamins, minerals and essential fatty acids. Add to a smoothie or use as a meal topper.

HERBS AND SPICES

Herbs and spices add more than just flavour; they are nutritious and have subtle healing properties when eaten over time.

Always try to use fresh herbs. They are rich in antioxidants and have many other health benefits. They're super easy to grow in little pots; you can snip some off, finely chop and mix into your dog's meal.

Spices have been used in Ayurvedic cooking for thousands of years. In Sanskrit, Ayurveda means 'the science of life'. Ayurvedic knowledge originated in India more than five thousand years ago and is often called 'the mother of all healing'.

Herbs and spices for your dog:

· Aniseed – has antibacterial, antifungal and anti-inflammatory properties.
· Cinnamon – has anti-inflammatory and antibacterial properties, regulates blood sugar levels, helps cognitive function and heart health, and settles the stomach.
· Fennel – aids digestion, helps with bloating and farting, and freshens stinky dog breath.
· Fenugreek – has excellent anti-inflammatory properties.
· Ginger – has anti-inflammatory and antibacterial properties, and aids digestion.
· Mint – freshens breath and aids digestion.
· Neem – has antibiotic and antifungal properties and is a powerful parasite repellent.
· Parsley – contains vitamin A, prevents bad breath and helps gut health.
· Rosemary – keeps skin and coat healthy.
· Sage – has antibacterial properties and is good for brain health.
· Turmeric – has powerful anti-inflammatory and antioxidant properties, boosts immunity, aids digestion and promotes brain and joint health.

FRUIT

Fruits are beneficial, anti-ageing food to add to your dog's diet. They contain fibre and vitamins A (as carotene) and C, and are low in fat and protein. They can be given as a healthy alternative to traditional treats, especially for overweight dogs, or added to meals. As with vegetables, moderation is key. Too much can cause digestive issues.

Most commercial fruit is treated with pesticides that can be toxic. Make sure you wash fruits and vegetables well before feeding them to your dog. Always cut fruit into bite-sized pieces.

Tip: Dried fruits – goji, blueberries and cranberries – are rich in antioxidants and anthocyanin.

FRUIT	NUTRITIONAL VALUE	MEAL SUGGESTIONS
Apple, seeds and core removed	Good source of vitamin C, fibre, calcium and phosphorus; promotes heart health and aids the digestive system	Duck with lentils and apple (page 115) Dog's pork roast (page 110)
Apricot, stone removed	High in antioxidants, beta-carotene and vitamins A, C and E; improves digestion and eye health	Cut the flesh into small pieces, and feed as an occasional treat or add to a meal
Banana	High in potassium, fibre, magnesium and vitamins B6 and C; supports heart health and helps regulate blood pressure. Feed in moderation as bananas contain a lot of sugar.	Add to Water kefir (page 126) as a frozen treat Banana peanut butter nice cream (page 133) Antioxidant-rich vegetable mash (page 83) Mash, stuff into a Kong and freeze as a treat
Blueberries	Filled with antioxidants including anthocyanin, vitamin C, fibre and phytochemicals; support the immune system	Bark (page 142) Vegan porridge (page 99) Water kefir (page 126) Granola-crackle bars (page 145) Blueberry and cinnamon brownie (page 149)

FRUIT	NUTRITIONAL VALUE	MEAL SUGGESTIONS
Cranberries	Contain potassium, fibre, vitamins A, B and E, and antioxidants; support the immune and urinary systems	Christmas cake (page 163)
Dragon fruit, outer shells removed	High in fibre, magnesium (which is known to boost low iron levels) and vitamins C and E; supports the immune system	Raw meal 1 (page 30)
Papaya, peeled	High in fibre, as well as vitamins A, B6, C, and E; aids gut health and supports the immune system	Dehydrate for treats (page 140) Duck with tapioca pearls and papaya (page 114)
Peach, stone removed	Great source of fibre, vitamin A, potassium, fluoride and iron; promotes healthy skin	Cut the flesh into small pieces, and feed as an occasional treat or add to a meal
Pear, core and seeds removed	Full of fibre and vitamins A and C; promotes gut and heart health Avoid tinned (canned) pears as they contain high amounts of sugar	Cut into small pieces, and feed as an occasional treat or add to a meal
Raspberries	High in fibre, potassium, manganese, copper, folic acid, iron, magnesium and vitamins B, C and K, and low in sugar and calories; reduce inflammation of the digestive system	Bark (page 142) Stress-busting smoothie (page 131)
Rockmelon (cantaloupe	Excellent source of dietary fibre, niacin, folate, potassium and vitamins A, B6 and C, and low in calories; supports the immune system and with its high water content prevents constipation	Cut the flesh into small pieces, and feed as an occasional treat or add to a meal

FRUIT	NUTRITIONAL VALUE	MEAL SUGGESTIONS
Strawberries	Full of antioxidants, high in fibre and vitamin C, and low in calories; support heart health and can help whiten teeth	Wash thoroughly and chop to add to a meal or smoothie or give as a treat
Watermelon, seeds and rind removed	Good source of potassium and vitamins A, B6 and C, and low in calories; supports the cardiovascular system	Watermelon gelato (page 132) Stress-busting smoothie (page 131)

OILS

Omega-3 fatty acids cannot be made by your dog's body so it is vital that you include them as part of their diet. Fish oils are the best source of essential fatty acids. The oils listed below provide essential fatty acids that help absorb vitamins. They're especially beneficial for dogs in the colder weather.

Tip: To keep oils in their peak condition store them away from light and heat, and preferably buy them in small quantities.

Oils for your dog:

· Avocado – high in omega-9 fatty acids that aid joint health and are good for the skin.
· Coconut – has beneficial fats that aid digestion. It contains lauric acid, which has antibacterial, antiviral and antifungal properties. It's a beauty food that works on the skin and coat, and it's easy to digest, which makes it great for the senior dog.
· Fish (such as salmon) – beneficial for the brain and immune system and promotes eye and bone health.
· Ghee (Indian clarified butter) – good for high-energy working dogs. Rich in fat-soluble vitamins A, D, E and K, ghee lubricates joints, boosts the immune system and aids brain and joint health. Only use in small quantities due to its high saturated-fat content.
· Hemp seed – contains omega-3 and other fatty acids as well as amino acids; it does not contain cannabidiol (CBD). It is good for the skin and coat.
· Linseed (flax seed) – good for the skin and coat.
· Olive – rich in antioxidants. Beneficial for the brain and the skin.
· Safflower – good for the heart and the immune system.
· Sunflower – good for the heart and for the skin.

HEMP CBD OIL

Cannabidiol (CBD) is a naturally occurring compound found in hemp and cannabis. CBD oil for dogs is derived from hemp and has no more than 0.3 per cent tetrahydrocannabinol (THC) or psychoactive properties, which makes it safe for dogs. Hemp CBD oil has been found to have a positive effect on dogs who are stressed and anxious, such as those who suffer from phobias or separation anxiety. It has also been shown to relieve pain, treat seizures and epilepsy, have anti-inflammatory properties and support the immune system.

In Australia, the UK and US, vets are allowed to prescribe off-the-shelf human CBD products to dogs as long as those products meet the standards of the relevant governing body. Buying the best CBD oil you can afford helps ensure that your dog will receive all of the benefits CBD oil has to offer.

Whether you're looking for a natural and safe alternative to regular medication or want to use CBD as a supplement to complement your dog's routine, you should consult with a vet before adding any hemp-derived CBD products to your dog's regime. Most importantly, your vet will recommend how much to give based on your dog's size and hold in mind any other medications your dog is taking.

ADD-ONS AND BEAUTY SUPERFOODS

It's best to add supplements at the time of feeding, rather than mixing them in ahead of time, because many of their nutrients are affected by freezing or by exposure to light or air. Depending on your dog's age, physical state and size, you can add between a teaspoon and a tablespoon of one or more of the following:

- Apple-cider vinegar – rich in antioxidants, lowers blood sugar levels, good for gut health and has antimicrobial and insect repellent properties.
- Brewer's yeast – rich in antioxidants and benefits digestive and skin health.
- Cottage cheese – good source of protein and calcium; a dairy product that dogs can usually tolerate.
- Fermented foods (kefir, kimchi, kombucha, sauerkraut) – a good source of probiotics that promotes a healthy immune system and helps fight harmful bacteria.
- Grains – support the immune system and good for the skin and coat.
- Kelp – rich in amino acids, iron and calcium, supports bone health, strengthens the immune system and aids in healing injuries.
- Legumes (such as sprouted lentils) – good source of fibre and protein when balanced with other ingredients.
- Full-fat Greek or plain yoghurt – good source of calcium and good fats; live active cultures provide probiotics that help digestion and gut health.

Tip: You can freeze probiotics such as Water kefir (page 126). Freezing causes the bacteria to enter a dormant state. Don't worry, bacteria are hardy little organisms and, when consumed or defrosted, will be alive and well.

Sprinkle some of nature's beauty goodness into your dog's meal:

- Aloe vera – soothes skin and has anti-inflammatory properties.
- Bee pollen – can be given daily; acts like a multivitamin and is good for dogs with skin allergies, especially in spring (½ teaspoon for a 30 kilogram/ 66 lb dog).
- Bilberry – full of antioxidants and great for eye health.
- Bran – rich in fibre and aids digestive health.
- Brewer's yeast – combats fleas and parasites.
- Hemp seeds – rich in protein, fibre, antioxidants and omega-3 and omega-6 fatty acids; great for your dog's heart, skin and joints.
- Lecithin – promotes a healthy coat.
- Maca powder – good for overall health.
- Neem – combats fleas and parasites.
- Quinoa flakes – gluten free and high in amino acids.
- Reishi mushrooms – support the immune system.
- Seaweed (kelp, nori, wakame) – contains selenium, iodine and zinc.
- Slippery elm – soothes the gut.
- Spirulina – contains selenium, iodine and zinc.
- Super greens – contain chlorella and barley grass.
- Tahini – good source of calcium.

NO-GO FOODS

- Alcohol (ethanol) – causes poisoning and depresses the nervous system.
- Avocado – the pip can obstruct your dog's windpipe and contains persin, a fungicidal toxin.
- Chocolate, cocoa powder, cacao beans – contains theobromine and caffeine, which are toxic and can be fatal for dogs. The darker the chocolate, the more fatal it is; cocoa, cooking chocolate and dark chocolate contain the highest levels of toxicity. Bottom line, if your dog has eaten a box of chocolates, contact your vet immediately.
- Caffeinated drinks (coffee, tea, energy drinks)
- Citrus – irritates the gut and nervous system.
- Cooked bones – can splinter and puncture your dog's throat and gullet.
- Corn on the cob – the husk can be a choking hazard and, if ingested, can lodge in the small intestine and lead to an intestinal blockage.
- Grapes (including raisins, sultanas) – although the reason is unknown, they can be fatal or lead to kidney failure.
- Greasy leftover meats – can cause diarrhoea and vomiting.
- Hops – can cause the body temperature to rise rapidly and malignant hyperthermia.

- Macadamia nuts – can cause vomiting and hyperthermia.
- Onions, leeks, chives (alliums) – can have a toxic effect and make your dog ill.
- Pips or seeds of fruit (e.g. apples, cherries, plums, peaches, watermelons)
- Raw dough – if it has yeast, it can ferment in the gut.
- Raw fish (e.g. salmon) – contains parasites that are deadly to dogs.
- Raw potato – contains a compound called solanine that is toxic for some dogs; when cooked, this is reduced.
- Rawhide – swells inside your dog's stomach and can get stuck in your dog's digestive tract.
- Sugar – your dog's digestive system cannot absorb sugar.
- Xylitol – an artificial sweetener found in diet products, chewing gum, toothpaste and food products such as peanut butter. Even a tiny amount of xylitol can be fatal – if a small dog eats even just two pieces of sugarless chewing gum, this can cause severe problems.

Tip: Instead of giving your dog rawhide, go for antlers or enrichment toys stuffed with treats (see page 138 for ideas).

Is a plant-based diet suitable for my dog?

If you are vegetarian or vegan, then feeding your dog a meat-free diet will be a natural progression of your own beliefs and ethics. It's commonly believed that dogs are carnivores like their wolf ancestors, but dogs are actually omnivores. Your dog's digestive system is quite capable of digesting and extracting nutrients from fruit and vegetables; it doesn't mind where its protein comes from – what matters is that the protein is complete, high quality, bioavailable and easily digestible.

We know that plants are great at providing antioxidants and vitamins, but what's really fantastic is that complete proteins can also be found in plants. High-quality proteins obtained from plant matter such as yeast, fungi, algae (like spirulina) and seaweed are complete proteins, meaning they contain the ten essential amino acids a dog needs to stay fit and healthy. Amino acids help build muscle, produce hormones and fight infection, which makes them a vital component of any balanced diet. Essential fatty acids (omega-3, omega-6 and omega-9) can also be found in plants and healthy oils and fats, such as avocado, canola, olive and linseed (flax seed) oils. These are common ingredients already found in your dog's food.

Not all vets agree that dogs can thrive on a plant-based diet and, to be honest, we are sceptical too. This is our personal view: dogs eat meat and need meat. Dogs have evolved from the wolf; raw meat was and is their natural diet. However, given the state of our planet, there is definitely a movement towards being kinder to it and concerns around the intensive farming of animals and the risk of pandemic outbreaks. For this reason we have consciously made many of our treat recipes vegan.

If you are planning to feed your pup a vegetarian or vegan diet, you have to be extremely diligent. Your pup will likely need extra supplements, including amino acids, L-carnitine and taurine to thrive. We recommend that you check with a vet or veterinary nutritionist before moving to a plant-based diet for your dog. A plant-based diet needs to be planned with expert care to make sure the dog is receiving the required nutrients. Greater consideration needs to be given for puppies, pregnant or nursing dogs and seniors before starting them on a plant-based diet.

Apply the same common sense as you do for your own diet. Do seek advice as recommended above, feed your dog a variety of foods and find out what works for your dog and what foods they like. Make meals that are nutritionally balanced, smell great and are appetising.

Foods to include in your dog's plant-based diet:

- Banana
- Brazil nuts
- Broccoli
- Carrot
- Herbal meal supplement (page 87)
- Kelp
- Lentils
- Oats
- Peanut butter
- Pinto beans
- Pumpkin
- Quinoa
- Soybeans

LINDA *from* MELBOURNE

How much should I feed my dog?

There is no one-size-fits-all method to figuring out how much to feed your dog. Your dog's breed, age, activity and general health are just some of the factors that you need to consider when working out a healthy portion size. For example, puppies need small, frequent feedings, whereas an adult dog should generally be fed twice a day. Portion sizes also depend on whether they're on a raw diet or having cooked meals because raw food tends to contain more water.

Our charts are rough guides based on weight (pages 72–73). The best way to avoid underfeeding or overfeeding your dog is to keep an eye on their body size and adjust their portions and diet accordingly. You can tell if your dog is at their ideal body weight by having a good look and feel of their body. They'll have a visible waist (when viewing their body from above) and their belly will tuck up between their ribs and hind legs (when viewing their body from the side). You'll be able to feel their ribs easily and note that there is minimal fat covering them.

JACQUI: A dog's weight can change quickly. I've adjusted Radar's meal size and seen the effects in as little as a week. The advantage of homemade dog food is that you can adjust your dog's diet and change the amount you feed and see the effects within a short amount of time. Increase or decrease the amount you feed your pup by around 10 per cent until you get a feel for what suits them best. Bear in mind that if your dog is active, they will need more food per day than a dog that is more of a couch potato. Each dog is an individual.

Our recipes have been designed with Fiona's dog, Holly, in mind. Holly is a medium-sized dog (17 kilograms/approx. 40 lb). You should scale your dog's portion sizes up or down accordingly. Remember, you know your dog best. You will know if they're getting enough food, or if they're eating too much or too little – just like you do with the rest of your family.

HOW TO WEIGH YOUR DOG

Most people weigh their dog at the vet, but you can also do it yourself. (However, if your dog is quite big, it may not be possible for you to do this safely.) Get some scales and first weigh yourself alone, then pick up your dog and weigh yourself again. The difference between the two measurements is your dog's weight.

UNDERWEIGHT

IDEAL

OVERWEIGHT

FEEDING GUIDELINES

SIZE CATEGORY	WEIGHT	DAILY AMOUNT
Toy	1.5 kg (3 lb)	⅓ cup
	3 kg (6 lb)	½ cup
Small	4.5 kg (10 lb)	¾ cup
	7 kg (15 lb)	1 cup
	9 kg (20 lb)	1⅓ cups
Medium	13.5 kg (30 lb)	1¾ cups
	18 kg (40 lb)	2¼ cups
	22.5 kg (50 lb)	2⅔ cups
Large	27 kg (60 lb)	3 cups
	32 kg (70 lb)	3½ cups
	36.5 kg (80 lb)	3¾ cups
	40 kg (90 lb)	4¼ cups
	45 kg (100 lb)	4½ cups

RAW FEEDING GUIDELINES

For raw meals, adult dogs should be fed meals that weigh 2 to 3 per cent of their ideal body weight while puppies should be fed 5 to 6 per cent of their ideal body weight.

IDEAL WEIGHT	RECOMMENDED DAILY AMOUNT	
	Adult	Puppy
5 kg (11 lb)	150 g (5½ oz)	300 g (10½ oz)
6–10 kg (13 lb–22 lb)	200 g (7 oz)	400 g (14 oz)
11–15 kg (24 lb–33 lb)	300 g (10½ oz)	600 g (1 lb 5 oz)
16–20 kg (35 lb–44 lb)	400 g (14 oz)	800 g (1 lb 12 oz)
21–25 kg (46 lb–55 lb)	500 g (1 lb 2 oz)	1 kg (2 lb 3 oz)
26–30 kg (57 lb–66 lb)	600 g (1 lb 5 oz)	1.2 kg (2 lb 10 oz)
31–35 kg (68 lb–77 lb)	700 g (1 lb 9 oz)	1.4 kg (3 lb 1 oz)
36–40 kg (79 lb–88 lb)	800 g (1 lb 12 oz)	1.6 kg (3½ lb)
41–45 kg (90 lb–99 lb)	900 g (2 lb)	1.8 kg (4 lb)
46–50 kg (101 lb–110 lb)	1 kg (2 lb 3 oz)	2 kg (4 lb 6 oz)

TINO *from* PARIS

Meals

Eating is one of our dog's greatest pleasures. We have created recipes that are delicious, healthy and inexpensive. Our recipes use real food and always include plenty of veggies because dogs need to eat their greens too.

Not only will your dog enjoy these meals, they will look and feel amazing too. Let us help take dog-bowl love to the next level!

IS YOUR DOG A CLOCK-WATCHER?

<u>JACQUI</u>: Radar is a massive clock-watcher. I swear he can tell the time. He will let me know in no uncertain terms when I am late with his dinner. He gets very hangry and a hangry Airedale terrier is no fun. For everyone's sake, when I know that we are going to be out, I pack him a complete meal, portioned and ready to eat. The result is that he is quieter, more settled and much, much happier, which means we are too. It also means that he won't get us up in the night for a poo or a wee, which is guaranteed to happen if he eats his dinner after 8 pm.

Base recipes

These recipes are great to have in your fridge or freezer. They're good to build meals from or to add to other meals, boosting their nutrition level and imparting extra flavour that your dog will love.

THE MANY BENEFITS OF BONE BROTH

· Bone broth is extremely nutritious – full of excellent protein and contains copper and iron.
· It helps digestion and liver function, and can reduce inflammation in the bowel.
· It provides electrolytes, rehydrates and is easy to digest. It adds moisture to a dog's diet.
· It protects the immune system.
· It promotes joint health as a good source of glucosamine and chondroitin.

This is an economical recipe. Instead of discarding the cooked frames after making your bone broth, you can use the cooked meat to prepare another meal base (see Chicken meal base).

Quick bone broth

Preparation time: 5 minutes
Cooking time: 3 hours
Makes: 1.5 litres (approx.
50 fl oz/6 cups)

1 kg (2 lb 3 oz) chicken bones
2 large carrots
4 celery stalks
1 bay leaf
2 parsley sprigs

Warm 3 litres (100 fl oz/12 cups) water in a large stockpot over a medium heat. Add all the ingredients and bring to a gentle simmer. Cook for 2 hours, skimming off any scum that comes to the surface.

Remove from the heat and strain the broth through a fine sieve. Discard the bones and vegetables, or set aside to make the bonus recipe below.

When cool, cover and chill in the fridge overnight until it sets like jelly. Use a tablespoon to scrape off any fat that has set on the top and discard. Portion into containers and refrigerate for up to 5 days or freeze for up to 3 months.

CHICKEN MEAL BASE

Pick off the cooked meat from the cooked frames, taking great care not to pull off any bones because they are sharp and can be dangerous for your dog to eat. Place the meat, carrots and celery in a food processor and blend to make a purée. Stir the purée through cooked brown rice or barley. Pack this down flat into freezer bags and store in the freezer for up to 3 months.

Liquid gold aka homemade bone broth. Bone broth is like medicine — so good for you and your dog, and simple to make.

It's good to use a mix of bones to ensure you get the beneficial properties found in each part of the animal. Marrow bones are full of valuable nutrients. Ask your butcher to cut the bone for you as described, so that it fits into your stockpot. Veal knuckles contain plenty of collagen. Chicken feet are a great source of cartilage — you can get them from your butcher or an Asian grocer.

Adding apple-cider vinegar will help extract the collagen from the bones, making the broth even more nutritious.

Bone broth

Preparation time: 5 minutes
Cooking time: 8—12 hours
Makes: 3 litres (approx.
100 fl oz/12 cups)

1 marrow bone, chopped
   into thirds and each third
   halved lengthways
1 veal knuckle (optional)
4 chicken feet
60 ml (2 fl oz/¼ cup) apple-
   cider vinegar
4 celery stalks
2 large carrots
2 parsley sprigs
2 bay leaves

Pour 4 litres (135 fl oz/16 cups) water into a large stockpot and add all the ingredients. Gently bring to the boil over medium heat, then simmer over a very low heat, preferably for 12 hours (or even up to 24 hours), making sure you don't let it boil dry. The longer the broth cooks, the more nutritious it will be.

Carefully remove from the heat and strain the liquid stock through a sieve into a large metal bowl. Discard the bones and vegetables.

When cool, cover and chill in the fridge overnight until it sets like jelly. Use a tablespoon to scrape off any fat that has set on the top and discard. Portion into containers and refrigerate for up to 5 days or freeze for up to 3 months.

Tip: Freeze some of this broth in ice-cube trays and add a bone-broth ice cube to your dog's evening meal.

Handy chickpea meal base

Preparation time: 5 minutes
Cooking time: 2 hours 15 minutes
Makes: 4 meal bases

1.1 kg (2 lb 7 oz/5 cups) dried chickpeas or 4 kg (8 lb 13 oz) tinned (canned) chickpeas
1 teaspoon Himalayan pink salt
3 teaspoons tahini
15 g (½ oz/¼ cup) nutritional yeast
1 bunch of parsley, chopped, including stalks, or herbs of your choice (optional)

If using dried chickpeas, soak them for at least 4 hours (or preferably overnight) in a generous amount of fresh water.

Drain and rinse the chickpeas well to wash away the carbohydrates and sugars that can cause flatulence. Cover the chickpeas with plenty of water in a large stockpot, bring to the boil and cook until soft, for about 1½ to 2 hours. Drain and mash well. Add in the salt, tahini, nutritional yeast and parsley (if using).

Store in individual portions in the fridge for up to 7 days or freeze for up to 3 months.

Sweet potato wedges

Preparation time: 5 minutes
Cooking time: 30 minutes
Makes: 9 side serves

550 g (1 lb 3 oz) sweet potato, peeled
45 g (1½ oz) coconut oil
1 tablespoon ground cinnamon
1 tablespoon ground turmeric

Preheat the oven to 160°C (320°F). Line a roasting tray with baking paper and set aside.

Chop the sweet potato into wedges and put in a large bowl.

Melt the oil gently in a microwave on medium heat or in a saucepan on the stove. Pour the oil evenly over the sweet potato wedges.

In a small bowl, mix the spices together. Massage the spice mixture over the sweet potato wedges with your hands. Transfer onto the roasting tray and bake for 30 minutes or until cooked.

Remove from the oven and serve when cool enough to eat. Store any remaining sweet potato, covered, in the fridge for up to 3 days.

This mash harnesses the nutritious power of yellow- and orange-coloured vegetables. Pair it with your dog's favourite protein and you're good to go.

Antioxidant-rich vegetable mash

Preparation time: 15 minutes
Cooking time: 1 hour 15 minutes
Makes: 8 meal bases

1 kg (2 lb 3 oz) butternut
   pumpkin (squash)
500 g (1 lb 2 oz) carrots
500 g (1 lb 2 oz) yellow
   zucchini (courgette)
1 yellow capsicum
   (bell pepper)
1 orange capsicum
   (bell pepper)
1 banana, peeled
1 tablespoon turmeric

Preheat your oven to 180°C (350°F). Line two baking trays with baking paper.

Wash the vegetables thoroughly. Cut the butternut pumpkin (squash) into roughly eight pieces, keeping the skin, pith and pips if you wish. Halve the carrots, zucchinis and capsicums.

Spread the vegetables over the prepared trays. Bake for 1 hour or until cooked thoroughly. Set aside to cool.

When cool, mash in a blender or food processor along with the banana and turmeric.

Store in the fridge for up to 7 days or in the freezer for up to 1 year.

Tip: To make into a complete meal, mix 200 g (7 oz) of the mash with 100 g (3½ oz) uncooked chicken hearts (roughly 10, straight from the freezer), 100 g (3½ oz) uncooked chicken livers (cut into quarters) and 2 uncooked chicken wings (chopped in half at the joint).

HEY PESTO!

Once you let your imagination go, there are plenty of things you can blend up in the food processor to make as doggie pesto. Mix 2 tablespoons of either pesto through cooked pasta and serve as part of a main meal or add a spoonful to any main meal. The Beetroot pesto can also be used as icing for cakes.

Beetroot pesto

Preparation time: 5 minutes
Makes: 400 g (14 oz)

200 g (7 oz) cooked beetroot
    (beets)
200 g (7 oz) cottage cheese
½ teaspoon ground fennel
1 tablespoon tahini
65 g (2¼ oz/⅔ cup) rolled oats

Blend all the ingredients in a food processor.

Transfer to a sealed container, scraping down the bowl using a spatula, and store in the fridge for up to 1 week.

Green pesto

Preparation time: 5 minutes
Makes: 190 g (6½ oz)

2 cups radish or spinach
    leaves, tightly packed
35 g (1¼ oz) unsalted cashews
60 ml (2 fl oz/¼ cup) olive oil
1 garlic clove
50 g (1¾ oz/½ cup) parmesan
    cheese
1 teaspoon spirulina

Blend all the ingredients in a food processor.

Transfer to a sealed container, scraping down the bowl using a spatula, and store in the fridge for up to 1 week.

This mayo will not only make your dog's meal look photo-worthy — it has a plethora of health benefits.

Apple-cider vinegar can help with kidney health, improve digestion, relieve arthritis and act as a natural insect repellent. Apple-cider vinegar is high in potassium as well as many other minerals.

Turmeric is especially good for ageing dogs; it helps ease joint pain, reduces osteoarthritis-related inflammation and improves brain health. Black pepper increases the bioavailability of the curcumin in turmeric.

Hemp seed oil is good for the heart and skin, and helps lower the risk of cancer. Hemp seeds are a good source of amino acids and healthy omega-3 and omega-6 fatty acids, and do not contain CBD.

Immune-boosting ginger mayo

Preparation time: 10 minutes
Makes: 200 ml (7 fl oz)

1 very fresh egg
1 tablespoon apple-cider
    vinegar
1 teaspoon turmeric
¼ teaspoon fresh ginger
pinch of black pepper
125 ml (4 fl oz/½ cup)
    hemp seed oil, or olive
    or sunflower oil

Using a food processor with the chopping blade fitted, pulse the egg for 20 seconds. Add the vinegar, turmeric, ginger and black pepper, and pulse again for 20 seconds. Scrape down the sides with a spatula.

Restart the processor and very slowly drip in the hemp seed oil, one drop at a time, until the sauce begins to thicken. If you like a runnier consistency, you can add a little water, one tablespoon at a time.

Store in a glass jar that has been thoroughly washed in hot, soapy water, and cover with a tight-fitting lid. Store in the fridge for up to 1 week.

This herbal meal supplement is packed full of goodness and smells amazing. It's not just for the fussy eater. Eggshells are the foundation of this supplement, being an excellent source of calcium, protein and phosphorus.

For an extra boost of protein and iron, blend in some Bark (page 142) or Lamb liver treats (page 141). You'll only need a little — about 8 cm × 5 cm (3¼ in × 2 in) segment — of either.

Note: Neem powder is available from health food stores and Indian grocery stores.

Herbal meal supplement

Preparation time: 5 minutes
Makes 500 g (1 lb 2 oz/2 cups)
(Suggested dosage is
⅛ teaspoon per 8 kg/18 lb of
dog weight)

6 eggshells, cleaned and dried
2 tablespoons kelp powder
1 tablespoon bran
1 tablespoon lecithin
1 tablespoon dried parsley
1 teaspoon dried sage
1 tablespoon ground fennel
1 tablespoon ground turmeric
1 tablespoon ground cinnamon
1 teaspoon neem powder
1 tablespoon sesame seeds
1 tablespoon sunflower seeds
1 tablespoon pepitas (pumpkin
  seeds)

Using a food processor with the chopping blade fitted, pulse all the ingredients except the seeds until well combined. Scrape down the sides with a spatula, then add the seeds and pulse until the mixture resembles a fine crumb.

Store in a glass jar that has been thoroughly washed with hot, soapy water, and cover with a tight-fitting lid. Keeps for 6 months in the pantry at room temperature.

Golden paste is a versatile recipe to have on hand and keeps well in the fridge for months. It's especially good in the winter months when cooler temperatures can induce arthritis or joint aches and pains. Mix in a spoonful with the evening meal or add to smoothies (see pages 129–131) or nice cream (page 133).

The turmeric is excellent in promoting both joint and brain health, making this recipe a good one for older dogs. Black pepper and coconut oil enhance turmeric's wonderful properties: the piperine in black pepper increases the bioavailability of curcumin in turmeric, while the coconut oil helps with absorption.

Golden paste

Preparation time: 5 minutes
Cooking time: 7 minutes
Makes: 330 ml (11 fl oz)

50 g (1¾ oz/¼ cup) turmeric
pinch of black pepper
70 g (2½ oz) coconut oil

Mix all the ingredients together with 180 ml (6 fl oz/¾ cup) water in a saucepan. Bring to the boil, then simmer for 5 minutes.

When cool, pour into a glass jar that has been thoroughly washed in hot, soapy water, cover and store in the fridge for up to 6 months.

Tip: Set the paste in little paw- or bone-shaped moulds for extra cuteness. Add one to the evening meal or freeze as a summer treat.

A nourishing milk for a rescue pup.

Emergency milk tonic

Preparation time: 2 minutes
Heating time: 2 minutes
Makes: 220 ml (7½ fl oz)

200 ml (7 fl oz) milk
1 egg yolk
1 tablespoon rolled oats
½ teaspoon brewer's yeast
1 teaspoon molasses

Gently warm the milk on a low heat; do not allow to boil. Remove from the heat and whisk in the egg yolk, oats and brewer's yeast, then, as the milk cools slightly, stir in the molasses.

Serve slightly warm or cold. Store in the fridge for up to 3 days.

FEEDING PUPPIES

Don't overfeed or overexercise a young pup. You don't want a pudgy puppy; keep them slightly hungry and slightly lean.

Puppies need good fats and high-energy foods, such as eggs, oats, yoghurt, brewer's yeast and sunflower oil.

Complete meals

Remember to only feed your dog raw meat that has been frozen first to reduce the bacteria that may be present in the meat.

Raw chicken dinner

Preparation time: 5 minutes
Makes: 1 meal

2 frozen chicken drumsticks
80 g (2¾ oz) cooked quinoa
½ teaspoon kelp powder
1 tablespoon cottage cheese
1 tablespoon chopped parsley
   or other fresh herbs
vegetable medley of your
   choice

Defrost the chicken drumsticks and chop into smaller pieces with a cleaver.

Add all the ingredients to a serving bowl and stir to combine.

<u>FIONA</u>: *I love making this recipe. I got the idea for it while having a chat with my butcher. I was buying three raw chicken frames for $3 to make stock and was telling her about how I patiently removed 750 grams (1 lb 11 oz) of meat from the frames when I last made stock. That's meat that would normally be tossed into the bin. When she responded, 'We put the raw frames through the mincer to make pet mince', I thought, 'Why don't I give that a go at home?'*

What I love about this recipe is that you know exactly what is in your pet mince and can rest assured that it definitely has no added fat.

You will need a food processor with a strong motor for this recipe; I use my trusty Thermomix, which did the job in 45 seconds. It's important to cut up the frame to help the food processor mince with ease.

DIY pet mince

Preparation time: 5 minutes
Makes: 2 meals

1 raw chicken or duck frame, chopped into quarters
1 rosemary sprig, leaves only
½ cup fresh parsley leaves, loosely packed
50 g (1¾ oz) carrot
40 g (1½ oz) zucchini (courgette)
125 g (4½ oz) beetroot (beet)
1 silverbeet (Swiss chard) leaf
½ apple, pips removed
95 g (3¼ oz/½ cup) cooked brown rice

Using a food processor with the chopping blade fitted, process the frame along with the herbs until the frame is minced. Add a little water or oil to help with the mincing process, if necessary. Scrape down the sides with a spatula, then add the carrot, zucchini and beetroot and continue to process for a further 30 seconds, scrape down and add the silverbeet leaf, apple and cooked rice, giving one final process until all combined.

Scrape the mixture out onto a plate with the spatula. Store covered in the fridge for up to 3 days or divide into meal portions and store in freezer bags in the freezer for up to 3 months. To save on freezer space, remove the air in the bags by flattening them and store them flat.

This is a great recipe to use in the first week of transitioning your dog from cooked meals to a raw diet — these meatballs can be served raw or lightly cooked. Fennel is also great for flatulence and tummy upsets.

Gently searing the meatballs not only creates more flavour for the fussy eater or the older dog but crisps up the oats to add extra texture.

Chicken and fennel meatballs

Preparation time: 10 minutes
Cooking time: 15 minutes
(optional — these meatballs can be served raw after they have been frozen and defrosted)
Makes: 7–8 meatballs

500 g (1 lb 2 oz) free-range chicken mince
80 g (2¾ oz/1 cup) coarsely grated carrot
80 g (2¾ oz/1 cup) shredded Tuscan cabbage
2 teaspoons ground fennel
1 handful parsley, roughly chopped
1 egg, whisked
250 g (9 oz/2½ cups) rolled oats
1 tablespoon olive oil, if cooking meatballs

Using a fork, combine all the ingredients except the oats and oil in a large bowl. Add 200 g (7 oz/2 cups) of the oats and continue mixing until thoroughly combined.

Spread the remaining oats onto a small tray. Divide the meatball mixture into portions of approximately 100 g (3½ oz) and, using your hands, shape each into a ball. Gently roll each ball in the prepared oats. Repeat until you have used up all of the mixture.

If cooking the meatballs, heat the oil in a frying pan over a medium heat and cook for 4–5 minutes or until lightly cooked through.

For dogs on a raw diet, first freeze the meatballs in an airtight container, then defrost before serving them.

The meatballs can be kept in the fridge for up to 3 days or in the freezer for up to 3 months.

Tip: To save on freezer space, make patties instead. Or freeze raw meatballs in a container first so that they hold their shape, then transfer them into a freezer bag. Lightly cooked meatballs can be stored immediately into a freezer bag when they are cool.

Garlic, ginger and turmeric have myriad health benefits. Garlic supports the immune system and can help combat fleas. Ginger and turmeric can help lower the risk of cancer. Ginger also helps to settle the stomach and relieve bloating while turmeric helps with arthritis.

Vietnamese pork meatballs

Preparation time: 10 minutes
Cooking time: 15 minutes
   (optional – these meatballs
   can be served raw after
   they have been frozen and
   defrosted)
Makes: 7 meatballs

500 g (1 lb 2 oz) pork mince
½ teaspoon crushed garlic
1 cm (½ in) fresh ginger, finely
   diced or grated
1 cm (½ in) fresh turmeric,
   finely diced or grated
1 tablespoon psyllium husks
1 egg, whisked
50 g (1¾ oz) grated carrot
2 outer iceberg lettuce leaves,
   finely shredded
1 pork kidney, roughly chopped
1 tablespoon chopped mint
1 tablespoon chopped parsley
185 g (6½ oz/1 cup) cooked
   brown rice
1 tablespoon olive oil, if
   cooking meatballs

Using a fork, combine all the ingredients except the oil in a deep bowl.

Divide the meatball mixture into portions of approximately 100 g (3½ oz) and, using your hands, shape each into a ball. Place them onto a clean tray.

If cooking the meatballs, heat the oil in a frying pan over a medium heat and cook the meatballs for 4–5 minutes or until lightly cooked through. Alternatively, you can cook the meatballs in the oven for 15 minutes at 170°C (340°F).

For a dog on a raw diet, first freeze the meatballs in an airtight container, then defrost before serving them.

The meatballs can be kept in the fridge for up to 3 days or in the freezer for up to 3 months.

Tip: You can easily replace the vegetables with others that you already have in your fridge. If you don't have fresh ginger or turmeric, use the ground spices instead.

This is an easy recipe that can be served raw or gently seared. Buy ready-made mince, or mince up your own meat in the food processor, and add in some offal for extra nutrition.

Beef burgers

Preparation time: 10 minutes
Cooking time: 12 minutes
  (optional — these burgers
  can be served raw after
  they have been frozen and
  defrosted)
Makes: 8 burgers

500 g (1 lb 2 oz) beef mince
1 tablespoon kelp powder
150 g (5½ oz/1 cup) cooked
  barley
1 cup finely chopped spinach
  leaves, loosely packed
1 zucchini, grated
1 egg, beaten
1 tablespoon olive oil, if
  cooking burgers
80 g (2¾ oz) cooked sweet
  potato to serve

Combine all the ingredients except the oil and sweet potato in a large bowl. Using your hands, shape the mixture into 8 burger patties and place them onto a plate.

If cooking the burgers, heat the oil in a frying pan over a medium heat and pan-fry the burgers. Cook for 6 minutes on each side. Cool before serving.

For dogs on a raw diet, first freeze the burgers in an airtight container, then defrost before serving them.

Top each serve with some sweet potato.

Store any remaining burgers in the fridge, covered, for up to 3 days or in the freezer for up to 3 months.

This is great for a dog that has been unwell or undernourished. It is full of iron and protein, and is very easy to digest, which makes it good for pregnant or feeding mumma dogs too.

Energy porridge

Preparation time: 5 minutes
Cooking time: 12 minutes
Makes: 320 g (11½ oz) or
1 large bowl

50 g (1¾ oz/½ cup) white
    quinoa
1 tablespoon olive oil
150 g (5½ oz/1 cup) frozen
    vegetables
40 g (1½ oz) cottage cheese
100 g (3½ oz) chopped liver

Bring 250 ml (8½ fl oz/1 cup) water to the boil in a small saucepan over a medium heat. Add the quinoa along with the oil, lower the heat and allow to simmer gently, covered, for around 10 minutes until the quinoa is fluffy.

Stir in the vegetables, followed by the cottage cheese. Finally stir through the liver, then turn off the heat and allow to stand, covered.

When the quinoa porridge has cooled slightly, pour into a bowl and serve.

This is a tasty porridge that's quick to prepare and is one that you can definitely share with your pup. Top the porridge with extra goodness — Brazil nuts have tons of selenium, while sesame seeds are packed with calcium and plant protein.

Vegan porridge

Preparation time: 5 minutes
Cooking time: 7 minutes
Makes: 240 g (8½ oz) or 1 bowl

1 tablespoon coconut oil
½ teaspoon ground cinnamon
50 g (1¾ oz/½ cup) rolled oats
1 teaspoon black chia seeds
1 tablespoon brewer's yeast
35 g (1¼ oz/⅓ cup) frozen
    blueberries
1 tablespoon Brazil nuts, finely
    chopped or ground to serve
1 teaspoon sesame seeds to
    serve

Heat a small saucepan over a medium heat and melt the coconut oil. Add the cinnamon, followed by the oats, and toast them, stirring occasionally, for 1½ minutes.

Add the chia seeds, then carefully pour in 250 ml (8½ fl oz/1 cup) water, watching that it doesn't spit all over. Next add the brewer's yeast and keep stirring. Finally add the blueberries and mix through.

Transfer to a bowl and serve when the porridge has cooled slightly. Top with the Brazil nuts and sesame seeds when ready to serve.

Tip: Porridge is great for toothless dogs, who are forced to lap up their food. Because doggie gums are more sensitive to extremes in cold and hot, serve the porridge at a warm temperature to avoid any discomfort. These porridge recipes can be made ahead of time and stored in the fridge for up to 3 days or in the freezer for up to 3 months. Warm in the microwave just before serving or, alternatively, serve it cold.

This is a cheat's version of a risotto. Not only is it tasty, it is also quick and easy to put together if you have cooked leftover brown rice and pumpkin (winter squash) in the fridge.

Beef and pumpkin risotto

Preparation time: 5 minutes
Cooking time: 25 minutes
Makes: 1 meal

1 tablespoon olive oil
350 g (12½ oz) beef or other meat, diced
½ teaspoon ground coriander
3 tablespoons cooked brown rice
1 cup shredded silverbeet (Swiss chard) leaves, tightly packed
100 g (3½ oz) liver, chopped
125 ml (4 fl oz/½ cup) stock
115 g (4 oz) pumpkin (winter squash) or sweet potato, roasted
2 tablespoons chopped parsley

Heat the oil in a medium non-stick pan over a medium heat. Add the diced beef and coriander and cook for 2 minutes, stirring with a wooden spoon. Add the rice, followed by the silverbeet and liver, and give them a good stir.

Pour in the stock, then add the pumpkin. Keep stirring the risotto until it comes together and all ingredients are lightly cooked.

Turn off the heat, add the chopped parsley and mix through.

Cool before serving.

This quick breakfast is plain but soothing. It's rich in magnesium and easy to digest.

Pumpkin and oat risotto

Preparation time: 5 minutes
Cooking time: 10 minutes
Makes: 1 meal

100 g (3½ oz/1 cup) rolled oats
500 ml (17 fl oz/2 cups) chicken
   broth
250 g (9 oz/2 cups) cooked
   pumpkin (winter squash)
1 tablespoon chopped parsley
1 tablespoon nutritional yeast
Greek yoghurt to serve
   (optional)

Gently toast the rolled oats in a heavy-based saucepan over a medium heat, stirring with a wooden spoon for a few minutes.

Carefully pour in the chicken broth, then continue to stir, bringing to a simmer. As the mixture thickens, add in the cooked pumpkin and mix through, followed by the chopped parsley and nutritional yeast.

Remove from the heat and cool in a serving bowl. Top with a dollop of Greek yoghurt, if using, when ready to serve.

JACQUI: When I was testing this recipe, my husband refused to taste it because he's funny about tofu. Pfft! It's delicious and jam-packed with goodness. If you're feeling adventurous, you can add a teaspoon of spirulina powder to the mix.

Meatless loaf

Preparation time: 15 minutes
Cooking time: 40 minutes
Makes: 4 meals

olive oil, for greasing and
   drizzling
280 g (10 oz) firm tofu, cut
   into cubes
2 slices wholemeal or
   sourdough bread, cut into
   cubes
165 g (6 oz/ 1⅔ cups) rolled
   oats plus extra, if necessary
3 tablespoons tamari or soy
   sauce
2 tablespoons nutritional yeast
2 tablespoons dijon mustard
¼ teaspoon ground black
   pepper
¼ teaspoon chopped garlic
1 tablespoon chopped parsley,
   including stalks
125 ml (4 fl oz/½ cup) low-salt
   tomato sauce
baked sweet potato to serve
green vegetables, such as
   cabbage, chopped kale,
   spinach or steamed broccoli
   to serve

Preheat oven to 150°C (300°F). Lightly oil a 25 cm × 13 cm (10 in × 5 in) baking tin.

Mix all the ingredients except the tomato sauce and vegetables with 375 ml (12½ fl oz/1½ cups) water in a large bowl until well combined. If the mixture is too dry, add a splash of water, or if too wet, add a sprinkle of rolled oats.

Spoon the mixture into the prepared tin. Top with tomato sauce and bake for approximately 40 minutes.

Cool the loaf before serving. Cut the loaf into 2 cm (¾ in) slices. Serve 2 slices as a meal topped with some sweet potato and green vegetables, and a drizzle of olive oil.

Store extra portions in the fridge for up to 7 days or in the freezer for up to 1 year.

Tip: You don't need a baking tin that is exactly 25 cm × 13 cm (10 in × 5 in) to make this recipe. You're aiming for the mixture to be at least 4 cm (1½ in) deep in the tin so it doesn't dry out. I sometimes spread the mixture between two smaller tins so that they store in the fridge and freezer more easily.

FIONA: *Whenever I make fresh juice, I put the veggies through the juicer first, so I can use the leftover pulp in Holly's meals. If I make a large batch of pulp, I make this delicious breakfast loaf — it's kind of a doggie frittata. The pulp I use has spinach, beetroot (beets), celery and ginger.*

I also serve this recipe raw. Every ingredient is perfectly fine for your dog to eat raw and will be nutritionally at its peak. When cooked, this loaf is a handy energy snack to take on a hike with your dog.

Adding the eggshells into the recipe will give it a calcium boost. You can also make this with feta, yoghurt or oat milk if you don't have any cottage cheese.

Veggie breakfast loaf

Preparation time: 10 minutes
Cooking time: 25 minutes
Makes: 6–8 slices
(1 slice per meal)

3 eggs, including shells
300 g (10½ oz) vegetable juice
  pulp
2 fresh rosemary sprigs, leaves
  only
200 g (7 oz/2 cups) rolled oats,
  plus 1 tablespoon extra for
  topping
2 tablespoons olive oil, plus
  extra for drizzling
200 g (7 oz/¾ cup)
  cottage cheese
1 tablespoon pepitas
  (pumpkin seeds)

Preheat the oven to 180°C (350°F). Line a 30 cm × 10 cm (12 in × 4 in) loaf tin with baking paper.

Crack the eggs into a bowl and set aside. If you'd like, whiz the eggshells in a food processor.

Using a food processor with the chopping blade fitted, pulse the vegetable pulp and the rosemary for 30 seconds to break down the tough strands of the vegetable fibre and chop the rosemary fully.

Add the oats, eggs, oil and cottage cheese, and pulse for another 30 seconds or until fully combined.

Spoon the mixture into the prepared tin, smoothing out the top with the back of a spoon or spatula. Sprinkle the top of the loaf with the pepitas and oats, then drizzle some olive oil over the loaf.

Bake in the oven for 25 minutes. Test with a wooden skewer; if it comes out clean and the loaf feels firm to the touch, remove from the oven and cool on a cooling rack.

When cool, slice the loaf into meal-sized portions for your dog (100 g/3½ oz slices per portion for a medium-sized dog). The loaf can be kept in the fridge, covered, for up to 3 days, or stored as single portions in freezer bags in the freezer for up to 3 months.

KUMO *from* CANBERRA

Tuna mac

Preparation time: 5 minutes
Cooking time: 10 minutes
Makes: 1 meal

150 g (5½ oz) tuna steak, fresh
   or defrosted
90 g (3 oz/½ cup) cooked
   pasta
75 g (2¾ oz/½ cup) frozen
   vegetables
1 tablespoon cottage cheese
½ teaspoon brewer's yeast
1 tablespoon chopped parsley
1 tinned (canned) sardine

In a small saucepan, cover the tuna steak with just enough water to poach. Poach for 6 minutes or until just cooked through.

Add the pasta and frozen vegetables and cook for 2 minutes, stirring the ingredients.

Drain the tuna and veggie pasta mix into a bowl. Chop the tuna into bite-sized cubes, then mix through the cottage cheese, brewer's yeast and parsley.

Top with a sardine just before serving.

Tip: Sprinkle a teaspoon of the Herbal meal supplement (page 87) over for a nutritional boost.

Cheat's dinner — you read that correctly! Maybe you didn't get out to the shops in time and have no fresh ingredients. Stuff happens and life can get in the way. Here is a quick, healthy meal made from pantry staples.

Cheat's dinner

Preparation time: 2 minutes
Makes: 1 meal

95 g (3½ oz) tinned (canned)
   tuna in olive oil
100 g (3½ oz) tinned (canned)
   black beans
100 g (3½ oz/1 cup) rolled oats
150 g (5½ oz/1 cup) frozen
   vegetables, defrosted
1 egg
1 teaspoon sesame seeds

Mix all the ingredients together in a bowl and serve.

Tip: Tinned (canned) products are handy for a quick, guilt-free meal for your dog. Look for ones with a high meat content and ingredients that you recognise and would eat yourself.

This is a no-fuss, super-fast dish to whip up, with all the flavours of a classic pork roast.

Dog's pork roast

Preparation time: 5 minutes
Cooking time: 10 minutes
Makes: 1 meal

1 tablespoon olive oil
180 g (6½ oz) pork, chopped
  into 3 cm (1¼ in) cubes
1 teaspoon ground sage
½ apple, seeds removed
  and chopped into 1–2 cm
  (½–¾ in) squares
100 g (3½ oz) liver, chopped
  in half
200 g (7 oz) cooked sweet
  potato
3 tablespoons (45 g/1½ oz)
  cooked lentils
40 g (1½ oz) broccoli, finely
  chopped

Heat oil in a medium non-stick pan over a medium heat. Add the pork, followed by the sage and apple. Stir with a wooden spoon for a couple of minutes, adding a little water, if needed, to help it come together.

Add the liver and cook for a further 3–4 minutes, allowing the mixture to simmer gently. Finally, add the sweet potato, lentils and broccoli, mixing everything together.

Remove from the heat and cool before serving.

Tip: Apples are an excellent fruit to feed your dog. They're a safe way to satisfy your pet's sweet tooth and dogs love the taste and the crunch. Chewing an apple can also help clean their teeth.

A quick mid-week meal that smells like a slow-cooked aromatic dish, thanks to its beautiful blend of healthy spices.

Middle Eastern lamb with pumpkin and barley

Preparation time: 5 minutes
Cooking time: 20 minutes
Makes: 1 meal

1 teaspoon olive oil
180 g (6½ oz) lamb shoulder, cubed
½ teaspoon ground cinnamon
½ teaspoon ground turmeric
½ teaspoon ground ginger
1 rosemary sprig, leaves only
½ red capsicum (bell pepper), seeds removed, chopped
125 ml (4 fl oz/½ cup) stock
100 g (3½ oz) beef heart, chopped
125 g (4½ oz/½ cup) roasted pumpkin (winter squash)
3 tablespoons cooked barley
Greek yoghurt to serve

Heat the oil in a medium non-stick pan over a medium heat. Add the lamb, spices, rosemary and red capsicum and stir quickly for 2–3 minutes.

Pour in the stock and allow to simmer for a few more minutes. Add the beef heart and stir.

Add the pumpkin and barley and mix through. Alternatively, add the pumpkin and barley just before serving.

Remove from the heat and cool before serving. Top with a tablespoon of Greek yoghurt and serve.

Tip: Don't overcook your dog's food because you'll lose some of the nutrients.

FEELING PAWLY

Sometimes having the same meal day in and day out can cause dogs to feel unwell, with issues affecting their skin or gut.

Chicken and beef are considered to be allergy-provoking, not because they contain more allergens than other meats but because they are the most common proteins fed to dogs. Enticing your pawly feeling pup to eat can be made easier by giving them a protein they have not tried before. Dogs are less likely to have a reaction to a protein they've not commonly eaten. Don't forget that Bone broth (page 81) can be made with lamb, venison, bison and rabbit too. Eggs are another great protein source for dogs that aren't feeling their best.

Like humans, scent plays a big part in encouraging your dog to eat so entice them with strong-smelling foods, such as offal, sardines and tinned (canned) tuna.

Tapioca pearls, oats and oatmeal are great alternatives to rice for dogs who are feeling under the weather. Always overcook starches, such as rice and pasta, to make them easier to digest.

Tip: Mix a little slippery elm with some cooked pumpkin (winter squash), sweet potato or a mashed-up boiled egg to help firm up loose stools.

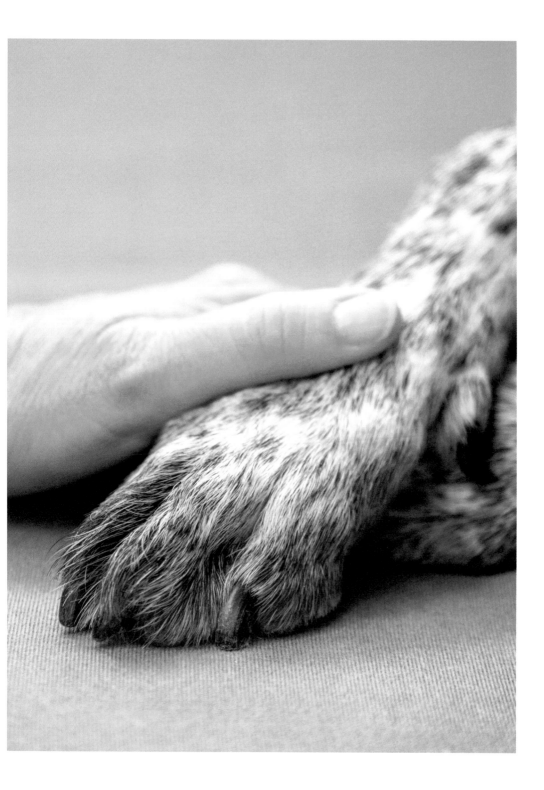

This recipe will make an ill pup feel better, with duck as a new protein, tapioca pearls to help firm up stools and a bit of slippery elm to settle the tummy. The papaya is a prebiotic that aids the good bacteria in the gut. Don't forget to include a teaspoon of the papaya seeds — they are highly nutritious and good for kidney health.

Duck with tapioca pearls and papaya

Preparation time: 10 minutes
Cooking time: 30 minutes
Makes: 1 meal

100 g (3½ oz/½ cup) tapioca
   pearls
1 duck breast, skin removed,
   or 300 g (10½ oz) rabbit
¼ teaspoon slippery elm
180 g (6½ oz) raw papaya,
   sliced

Cook the tapioca pearls following the instructions on the packet. When cooked, set aside.

Meanwhile, put the duck in a saucepan, cover with water and poach for 15 minutes. Carefully remove the duck and, when cool, chop into small pieces. Mix the tapioca pearls and slippery elm through. Add the papaya just before serving.

Duck contains antioxidants that help boost the immune system and regulate normal thyroid function. The omega-3 fatty acids in duck meat also help your dog maintain a healthy coat.

Duck with lentils and apple

Preparation time: 5 minutes
Cooking time: 15 minutes
Makes: 1 meal

1 duck breast, skin removed
½ carrot
3 brussels sprouts, cut in half
½ apple, seeds removed
90 g (3 oz) cooked lentils
1 parsley sprig, chopped

Put the duck breast in a heavy-based saucepan with at least 125 ml (4 fl oz/½ cup) water to cover. Add the carrot, brussels sprouts and apple and poach gently for 10–15 minutes.

Turn off the heat and remove the duck, carrot, brussels sprouts and apple from the stock. Slice the duck and chop the carrot, brussels sprouts and apple, and put in a serving bowl.

Add the cooked lentils to the serving bowl and pour the stock over. Mix in the parsley and serve.

This flavoursome slow-cooked dish is handy as a freezer meal for later. You can swap the pumpkin and fennel for other seasonal vegetables.

Slow-cooked brisket with Mediterranean vegetables

Preparation time: 5 minutes
Cooking time: 4 hours
Makes: 4 meals

1 kg (2 lb 3 oz) piece of brisket
2 carrots
3 celery stalks
1 rosemary sprig
1 tablespoon vegetable stock powder
400 g (14 oz) pumpkin (winter squash), chopped
500 g (1 lb 2 oz) fennel bulb, cut into quarters
175 g (6 oz/1 cup) cooked quinoa

Put the brisket, carrots, celery, rosemary and stock powder into a large heavy-based stockpot and pour in enough water to cover the meat. Cover and bring to the boil over a medium heat. Gently simmer, covered (this makes sure it doesn't dry out), for 4 hours or until the meat is tender and cuts through like butter; in the last 30 minutes of cooking, add the pumpkin and fennel. Add more water if needed. Remove from the heat when the pumpkin and fennel are cooked.

Allow the brisket and vegetables to cool in the fridge. When cool, using tongs, remove the brisket and vegetables from the stock and slice. Stir in the quinoa and serve.

To store, divide into single-meal portions (with about 2 tablespoons of quinoa each portion). Store in the fridge for up to 3 days or in the freezer for up to 3 months.

Tip: Serve each meal with 50 ml of stock, if you'd like.

This one-pot meal has a heavenly, sweet-smelling golden stock full of spices. You could add other root vegetables to this aromatic dish. Use a pressure cooker to halve the cooking time.

Moroccan lamb hotpot with freekeh

Preparation time: 5 minutes
Cooking time: 1 hour, or 30 minutes in a pressure cooker
Makes: 2 meals

400 g (14 oz) lamb neck
1 teaspoon ground cinnamon
1 teaspoon ground turmeric
1 bay leaf
1 parsley sprig
1 large potato, cut in half
170 g (6 oz/1 cup) freekeh
100 g (3½ oz) liver, chopped

Put all the ingredients except the liver into a large stockpot or into a pressure cooker. Pour in approximately 2 litres (68 fl oz/8 cups) water and cook for 1 hour on the stovetop or 30 minutes in the pressure cooker.

At the end of the cooking time, add the liver. The heat will cook the liver in a matter of seconds.

Using tongs, place the lamb neck, liver and potato onto a plate. When cool enough to handle, remove the lamb meat from the bone using a sharp knife. Discard the bone.

Using a sieve, carefully drain the stock into a bowl, reserving the cooked freekeh. Allow the stock to cool.

To plate up, put the meat in a serving dish with the potato and some freekeh. Top with a cup of stock.

Tip: Reserve the golden stock to make iced treats for later — it's too good to throw away. Just pour into some icy pole moulds (popsicle molds) and freeze until set.

This is one healthy pie. The combination of parsley and nori is great for your dog's gums and oral health. You could replace the potato with pumpkin (winter squash) or sweet potato, or whatever vegetables you may have on hand.

Fishy bean pie

Preparation time: 20 minutes
Cooking time: 1 hour
Makes: 2 meals

cooking oil to grease
    baking dish
335 g (12 oz) potatoes
300 g (10½ oz) frozen basa
    fillet or fish fillet of your
    choice
1 teaspoon fish stock (optional)
handful of fresh herbs, such
    as rosemary, parsley and
    bay leaves
100 g (3½ oz) cooked
    kidney beans
1 tablespoon parsley, roughly
    chopped
1 egg, beaten
1 tablespoon crushed nori
    sheet
1 teaspoon coconut oil
    (optional)

Preheat the oven to 170°C (340°F). Lightly oil a 26 cm × 16 cm (10 in × 6 in) baking dish and set aside.

Peel the potatoes and chop into quarters. Place in a saucepan, cover with water and bring to the boil. Simmer for 15 minutes or until cooked through. Carefully drain off the water and mash the potatoes using a potato masher, adding a little extra water, if necessary, to assist the mashing process. Set aside.

In another saucepan, cover the fish fillets with just enough water. Add in the fish stock, if using, and herbs. Warm over a gentle heat and poach for a few minutes until the fillets are translucent.

Turn off the heat, carefully remove the fillets and put them in a bowl, then add the kidney beans, parsley and egg. Stir gently with a spoon to combine.

Spoon the mixture evenly into the prepared baking dish. Top with the mashed potato, sprinkle with crushed nori and dot with small knobs of coconut oil, if using.

Bake in the oven for 40 minutes or until the potato crust begins to go golden around the edges.

Remove the pie from the oven and allow to cool before serving.

The pie can be stored, covered, in the fridge for up to 3 days or stored in a freezer bag in the freezer for up to 2 months.

PENNY *from* MELBOURNE

Treats

Who's treating who here? It's definitely your dog getting that mouth-watering treat. From dehydrating single ingredients for high-value training treats to making refreshing iced treats and smoothies for gut health, this chapter has your dog covered.

It is always important to factor the number of treats into your dog's overall diet. Don't go overboard, because your dog won't be telling you to stop. Treats should make up no more than 10 per cent of your dog's daily diet.

This is a super-quick energy icy pole (popsicle) for your dog to enjoy after a big beach run. It's important not to add too much Vegemite because it is high in sodium.

Vegemite iced treat

Preparation time: 5 minutes
Freezing time: 5 hours
Makes: 9 icy poles (popsicles)
(using 65 ml/2¼ fl oz icy pole moulds/popsicle molds)

1 teaspoon Vegemite or
   Marmite or Promite

Boil 600 ml (20½ fl oz) water and pour into a jug, then add the Vegemite. Use a whisk to combine, then allow to cool.

Pour into the icy pole moulds (popsicle molds) and set in the freezer for 5 hours.

Yes, shop-bought juice makes for an easy iced treat that is packed full of vitamins and minerals.

V8 iced treat

Preparation time: 5 minutes
Freezing time: 5 hours
Makes: 9 icy poles (popsicles)
(using 65 ml/2¼ fl oz icy pole moulds/popsicle molds)

600 ml (20½ fl oz) V8 juice or
   other vegetable juice

Simply pour the juice into the icy pole moulds (popsicle molds) and set in the freezer for 5 hours.

Take bone broth to the next level with goji berries and chia seeds. Did you know the other name for goji berry is wolfberry? Goji berries have immune-boosting properties and can help lower the risk of cancer. They are also great for your dog's skin. Chia seeds help brain health and are packed with omega-3.

Bone broth iced treat

Preparation time: 5 minutes
Freezing time: 5 hours
Makes: 7 icy poles (popsicles)
(using 65 ml/2¼ fl oz icy pole
moulds/popsicle molds)

500 ml (17 fl oz/2 cups) Bone
    broth (page 81)
1 tablespoon black chia seeds
1 tablespoon goji berries

Gently heat the broth in a saucepan over a medium heat, then add the chia seeds and stir.

Once the broth comes to the boil, turn off the heat. Allow to cool.

Meanwhile, place a few goji berries at the bottom of each icy pole mould (popsicle mold), then carefully top with the chia bone broth. Set in the freezer for 5 hours.

We've all heard about the goodness of kombucha, but why not try making some water kefir for you and your pup? Kefir is a versatile culture that can be used to ferment any carbohydrate-rich liquid.

The culture is a symbiotic community of bacteria and yeast (also known as a SCOBY) that looks like small translucent white granules that multiply when fed. Water kefir is a naturally fizzy drink that is great for your gut and your dog's gut. Don't worry about the sugar content in the recipe: the kefir grains will consume most of the sugar during the fermentation process. You will end up with a pleasantly bubbly drink, a bit like soft drink but without all the nasty stuff. It is also vegan.

Note: Kefir grains can be purchased online.

Water kefir

Probiotic drink

Preparation time: 5 minutes
Fermenting time: 24 hours
Makes: approx. 1 litre
(34 fl oz/4 cups)

950 ml (32 fl oz) filtered or
    cool boiled water
210 g (7½ oz/¼ cup) organic
    cane sugar
60 g (2 oz/¼ cup) kefir grains

If you don't have a water filter, boil your water and leave it to cool – ideally for 12 hours – before using. This will allow the chlorine to evaporate from the water.

Begin with a clean jar that can hold at least 1 litre of liquid. Fill half the jar with the water, then add the sugar and stir until it dissolves.

Add the kefir grains, followed by the rest of the water. Top the jar with a piece of clean kitchen roll or muslin and secure with an elastic band. Leave on your benchtop, out of direct sunlight, for at least 24 hours, but no more than 7 days.

Strain the kefir into a bottle or jar and put in the fridge. Your water kefir is now ready to drink.

Leave the grains in your fermenting jar and repeat the process to make more. You will notice that the grains will multiply. In time, you should move them into a larger jar or split the grains to start a second batch.

JACQUI: Slosh the water kefir straight onto your dog's meal. For a bit of fun, add a few fresh blueberries or sliced banana to large ice-cube moulds, then pour about 50 ml (1¾ fl oz) of water kefir into each and freeze. This is Radar's favourite ice-cube treat; he loves them and so does his little pug pal Phoebe.

PROBIOTICS VS PREBIOTICS

Probiotics are the bacteria themselves, so adding them directly increases the number of good bacteria. Examples of probiotics include fermented foods such as green tripe, kefir, yoghurt and sauerkraut. Probiotics help balance the gut flora.

Prebiotics, such as aloe vera and chicory, are essentially food for the good bacteria; they are non-digestible foods that make their way through the digestive system and help good bacteria grow and flourish. Adding prebiotics enables the probiotics to thrive and increase in number.

The goal of consuming both probiotics and prebiotics is to improve the number of good bacteria in the gut to aid digestion.

Papaya is a great prebiotic for gut health, while neem has antibacterial and antifungal properties.

Note: Neem powder is available from health food stores and Indian grocery stores.

Gut health smoothie

Preparation time: 5 minutes
Makes: 375 ml (12½ fl oz/
1½ cups)

100 g (3½ oz) papaya, peeled
 (including seeds)
2 tablespoons Greek yoghurt
1 egg
1 teaspoon psyllium husks
1 teaspoon sesame seeds
185 ml (6 fl oz/¾ cup) oat milk
¼ teaspoon neem powder

Pulse all the ingredients together in a blender until fully combined.

Serve immediately, storing the remainder in the fridge, covered, for up to 3 days. You can also freeze the surplus in ice-cube trays, covered with plastic wrap.

GUT HEALTH

To improve gut health (especially after a long treatment of antibiotics, period of stress or weight loss), add some of these ingredients in your dog's diet:

- Aloe vera
- Chicory
- Fennel
- Psyllium husk
- Slippery elm

Herbs like slippery elm and fennel help soothe and protect the gastrointestinal tract, improve stool consistency and reduce your pup's farts. They are also great to add when your dog is transitioning to a new diet.

JACQUI: Fermented foods, such as kefir, sauerkraut and kombucha, can be great for gut health. I have sloshed some kombucha on Radar's meals and he doesn't mind it. I guess it's the same as adding apple-cider vinegar.

Tip: Flatulence issues? Carbs are the biggest culprit. Switching to a natural diet will help.

The ultimate antioxidant smoothie! Omega oils are essential for skin and coat quality, heart health, immune response, brain function and mobility. Research has shown that DHA from fish oils makes puppies more intelligent and easier to train — it also improves their memory. Goat's milk is especially good for puppies because it helps support their digestive and immune systems.

Rich omega-3 shake

Preparation time: 5 minutes
Makes: 250 ml (8½ fl oz/1 cup)

125 g (4½ oz) tinned (canned)
    sardines
1 egg
2 tablespoons Greek yoghurt
125 ml (4 fl oz/½ cup) goat's
    milk
1 tablespoon hemp seeds
1 tablespoon chopped parsley
80 ml (2½ fl oz/⅓ cup) aloe
    vera juice

Pulse all the ingredients together in a blender.

Serve immediately, storing the remainder, covered, in the fridge for up to 3 days. You can also freeze the surplus in ice-cube trays, covered with plastic wrap.

Did you know that quinoa is a super grain? It's different from other grains in that it's a complete protein. It's also an excellent source of iron, calcium, potassium, B vitamins, magnesium and zinc. This smoothie is a mega dose of vitamins and minerals.

Immune-boosting green smoothie

Preparation time: 5 minutes
Makes: 250 ml (8½ fl oz/1 cup)

½ frozen zucchini (courgette)
1 cup spinach leaves, firmly
    packed
1 stalk celery, chopped
1 pear, pips and stalk removed
¼ teaspoon nutmeg
2 tablespoons quinoa flakes
1 teaspoon kelp powder
handful of fresh mint and
    parsley leaves

Pulse all the ingredients together in a blender, adding a little water if it is too thick.

Serve immediately, storing the remainder in the fridge, covered, for up to 3 days. You can also freeze the surplus in ice-cube trays, covered with plastic wrap.

Get your dog to load up on magnesium and vitamins B and C with this smoothie. The oats help soothe the nervous system.

Stress-busting smoothie

Preparation time: 5 minutes
Makes: 750 ml (25½ fl oz/
3 cups)

300 g (10½ oz) watermelon,
    chopped
60 g (2 oz/½ cup) raspberries
1 tablespoon chia seeds
1 teaspoon ground cinnamon
1 teaspoon brewer's yeast
50 g (1¾ oz/½ cup) rolled oats

Pulse all the ingredients together with 250 ml (8½ fl oz/1 cup) water in a blender.

Serve immediately, storing the remainder in the fridge, covered, for up to 3 days. You can also freeze the surplus in ice-cube trays, covered with plastic wrap.

This is the essence of summer and is beautiful in a celebration spread. Everybody loves watermelon, even dogs. Watermelon is a health-food powerhouse packed with nutrients — potassium and vitamins A, B6 and C — and low in calories. Be sure to remove the seeds and avoid giving your dog the rind because it can upset their stomach.

Ginger is great for settling tummy upsets or inflammatory issues. Brewer's yeast is rich in vitamin B, alleviates skin and coat issues and naturally repels fleas, ticks and mites.

Watermelon gelato

Preparation time: 5 minutes
Makes: 450 g (1 lb)

1 teaspoon grated fresh ginger
450 g (1 lb/3 cups) frozen
   chopped watermelon
1 teaspoon chopped fresh mint
1 teaspoon brewer's yeast

Use a food processor with the chopping blade attached or a Thermomix to whip this up. First mince the ginger for a few seconds, then add the remaining ingredients.

Spoon out and serve immediately; otherwise transfer to freezer containers and store for up to 2 months in the freezer.

Tip: Always have some frozen chopped watermelon on hand so you can make this delicious recipe in an instant, even for the humans. If you'd like a bit of alcohol, just add some vodka to the mix.

The high level of potassium in bananas makes them a great food for your dog; potassium is essential for maintaining an optimal fluid balance in the body.

Banana peanut butter nice cream

Preparation time: 5 minutes
Makes: 300 g (10½ oz)

115 g (4 oz/1 cup) ice cubes
1 frozen banana
60 g (2 oz/½ cup) frozen
  chopped zucchini (courgette)
  or frozen peas or broccoli
1 tablespoon peanut butter
2 tablespoons Greek yoghurt
1 teaspoon ground cinnamon

Pulse the ice in a food processor with the chopping blade fitted or in a blender until the ice becomes a fine iced crumb consistency. Add the remaining ingredients and process until combined, with the consistency of ice cream.

Transfer to a freezer container. Serve a scoop immediately, then store the remaining nice cream in the freezer for up to 2 months.

Golden paste nice cream

Preparation time: 5 minutes
Makes: 300 g (10½ oz)

115 g (4 oz/1 cup) ice cubes
1 frozen pear, pips, core and
  stalk removed
2 tablespoons Greek yoghurt
2 tablespoons Golden paste
  (page 88)

Pulse the ice in a food processor with the chopping blade fitted or in a blender until the ice becomes a fine iced crumb consistency. Add the remaining ingredients and process until combined, with the consistency of ice cream.

Transfer to a freezer container. Serve a scoop immediately, then store the remaining nice cream in the freezer for up to 2 months.

Tip: Alternatively store your nice cream as individual servings, using either icy pole moulds (popsicle molds) or little 50 g (1¾ oz) freezer containers.

Enrichment

SIMPLE WAYS TO MAKE YOUR DOG'S DAY AND STOP THEM FROM GETTING BORED

- Teach your dog a new trick.
- Hold 5-minute training sessions.
- Set up a safe DIY obstacle course for agility training.
- Play hide-and-seek (see page 137).
- Allocate digging space for your dog if they love to dig.
- Take your dog on a hike.
- Get your dog to do some nose work by hiding some treats around the room or house.
- Give your dog some homemade food puzzles (see page 138).
- Stuff some food into a toy (e.g. a Kong) for your dog (see page 139 for recipes).
- Give your dog a good meaty bone to chew – it'll provide great mental and physical stimulation.
- Make your dog a refreshing snack, such as the Vegemite or V8 iced treats (page 124).
- Treat your dog to a spa or massage.
- Provide your dog with a snuggle mat.
- Put on a dog video – some dogs love watching dog videos as much as we do.

Tip: Train your dog with a high-value treat, such as Lamb liver treats (page 141). Reward them when they get a trick right or when they navigate successfully through an obstacle course.

HIDE-AND-SEEK

Teach your dog to play hide-and-seek. It's a fun workout for their brain and body.

STEP 1

Let your dog see you hide. Talk excitedly to them while you hide.

STEP 2

Ask your dog to 'find' you. Your dog will come to you, using their sense of sight because they saw where you hid. This establishes the game. Reward them with praise.

STEP 3

Do not let your dog see you hide. Let your dog search, using their sense of smell, hearing and sight to guide them to you.

STEP 4

Increase the distance and the complexity of your hiding spots. Ignore your dog when they're off track. When your dog finds you, reward them with play and attention.

STEP 5

Start substituting yourself for another person. Get them to hide while you direct your dog to 'find' them. Reward your dog for finding the new player.

STEP 6

Continue to practise, using the word 'find' as a cue. Increase the distance and complexity of your hiding spots each game. Have multiple people hide. It just adds to the fun.

HOMEMADE FOOD PUZZLES

Get your dog to work for their food by creating some easy homemade puzzles. Not only will this slow down your dog's eating but it will also alleviate boredom and provide entertainment both for your dogs and their human pals.

BOXES
Put treats in a box and close it. Add difficulty by putting boxes inside boxes, with treats in between each layer.

MUFFIN TIN
Turn a muffin tin upside down and spread treats or your dog's food between the bumps. Your dog will have to nudge at the food from different angles to eat it. The top of the tin is flat, so they can't just flip it over; this is a great option for larger dogs.

TOWEL OR BLANKET
Simply spread your dog's treats out under a towel on the floor. Let your dog sniff around and find all of the pieces. You can also hide treats in the cushions of your sofa, or around your house, for added difficulty.

TENNIS BALL
An old tennis ball can be turned into a puzzle. Cut along the seam to make a flap. Stuff some treats inside and let them go for it.

PLASTIC BOTTLES
First of all, please don't try this if you have a dog who eats plastic. Unscrew the bottle top, put some treats inside, then screw the top back on. Your dog will figure out how to remove the top and their reward will be accessing the treats inside.

JACQUI: Radar loves food puzzles. He loves to shred cardboard boxes – it's a great de-stress activity for him. (He never eats the pieces; he spits them out.)

Radar also loves plastic bottles, but his enthusiasm for them does mean that he harasses me (and anyone else for that matter) for empty bottles.

Salmon is a good source of omega-3 and is incredibly tasty. Stuff this pâté into food toys (such as Kongs) to keep your pup from getting bored.

Salmon pâté

Preparation time: 5 minutes
Makes: 615 g (1 lb 6 oz/3 cups)

415 g (14½ oz) tinned (canned)
   wild pink salmon
200 g (7 oz) cottage cheese
1 teaspoon chopped fresh
   rosemary or ¼ teaspoon
   dried rosemary

Drain the liquid from the tin of salmon. Keep the bones, because they are edible, soft and a source of added calcium.

Using a food processor with the chopping blade fitted, blend all the ingredients until smooth.

Store in the fridge, covered, for up to 3 days or store in a freezer bag in the freezer for up to 2 months.

Here's another quick stuffing to whip up so your dog gets variety.

Sardine pâté

Preparation time: 5 minutes
Makes: 415 g (14½ oz/1⅔ cups)

215 g (7½ oz) tinned (canned)
   sardines
200 g (7 oz) cottage cheese
1 teaspoon dried sage

Drain the liquid from the tin of sardines. Keep the bones, because they are edible, soft and a source of added calcium.

Using a food processor with the chopping blade fitted, blend all the ingredients until smooth.

Store in the fridge, covered, for up to 3 days or store in a freezer bag in the freezer for up to 2 months.

Dehydrated vegetables make healthy training treats. Raw vegetables are great too, but always remember to cut them finely for easy digestion.

Experiment with other vegetables and fruits such as sweet potato, beetroot (beets), coconut and papaya.

Carrot treats

Preparation time: 5 minutes
Dehydrating time: 4–8 hours
Makes: 1 cup

4 large carrots

Preheat the oven to 100°C (210°F). Line a baking tray with baking paper.

Finely slice the carrots into 5 mm (¼ in) slices or cut them using a food processor with the fine-cutting blade fitted.

Arrange the sliced carrots evenly on the prepared tray. Place the tray on the bottom shelf in the oven and cook for 8 hours or until crispy. Alternatively, place in a dehydrator and follow its instructions for dehydrating vegetables.

Before storing, check that the carrots are completely dried out. Store in an airtight container for up to 2 months.

Tip: To make a natural coloured icing with no nasties, whiz some dehydrated carrots up to a fine powder in a food processor with the chopping blade fitted. Add a spoonful to the Fudge icing recipe (page 167) for a pretty apricot colour.

This is a high-value training treat that your dog won't mind working for. It's also great for decorating the Party cake (page 157) or Turmeric panettone (page 150).

Lamb liver treats

Preparation time: 10 minutes
Dehydrating time: 6–12 hours
Makes: 240 g (8½ oz)

700 g (1 lb 9 oz) lamb livers

Preheat the oven to 100°C (210°F). Line a baking tray with baking paper.

Using a food processor, pulse the livers with 50 ml (1¾ fl oz) water until combined. Add a little more water if still gluggy, and pulse to combine.

Using a spatula, spread the liver purée evenly onto the prepared tray, taking care not to spread too close to the edges.

Place the tray on the bottom shelf in the oven and cook for 12 hours. Alternatively, place in a dehydrator for 6 hours.

Before storing, check that the liver purée is completely dried out. Break into shards and store in an airtight container for up to 3 months. These are best stored in the fridge.

OTHER EXCELLENT DEHYDRATED OFFAL

- Chicken necks – once dehydrated, chop into bite-sized treats; leaving them whole can be a choking hazard for a dog that does not chew their food.
- Chicken hearts – the perfect treat size!
- Lamb kidneys – dehydrate the kidneys whole in the oven for 4–5 hours (or 2 hours in a dehydrator), then slice them into 1 cm (½ in) slices.

This is another high-value treat your pup will love. It's also pretty and can be used to decorate cakes.

Bark

Preparation time: 10 minutes
Dehydrating time: 8–12 hours
Makes: 160 g (5½ oz)

600g (10½ oz) chicken livers, puréed
1 tablespoon dried blueberries
1 tablespoon sunflower seeds
1 tablespoon pepitas (pumpkin seeds)
1 tablespoon shredded coconut
1 tablespoon freeze-dried raspberries

Preheat the oven to 100°C (210°F). Line a baking tray with baking paper.

Using a spatula, spread the liver purée evenly onto the prepared tray, taking care not to spread too close to the edges. Sprinkle all the other ingredients over the top.

Place the tray on the bottom shelf in the oven and cook for 12 hours. Alternatively, place in a dehydrator for 8 hours.

Before storing, check that the liver purée is completely dried out. Break into shards and store in an airtight container in the pantry for up to 2 months.

Pumpkin pie biscotti

Preparation time: 5 minutes
Chilling time: 30 minutes
Cooking time: for soft biscotti,
  30 minutes; for crunchy
  biscotti, 1 hour
Makes: 12 biscuits

135 g (5 oz/½ cup) cooked
  pumpkin (winter squash)
1 egg, lightly beaten
2 teaspoons ground ginger
1 teaspoon ground cinnamon
200 g (7 oz/1⅓ cups) plain
  (all-purpose) flour
75 g (2¾ oz) pepitas (pumpkin
  seeds), plus extra — roughly
  chopped for sprinkling
80 g (2¾ oz) carob buttons
2 tablespoons coconut oil, plus
  extra if needed

In a medium bowl, mash the pumpkin with a fork. Mix in the egg, followed by the spices and flour. Finally, mix in the pepitas.

With clean hands, knead the dough in the bowl for a few minutes or until it comes together and is smooth. The pepitas will be speckled throughout the dough. Turn the dough out onto a floured bench and roll into a 20 cm (8 in) long sausage. Wrap in plastic wrap and chill in the fridge for 30 minutes.

Preheat the oven to 175°C (345°F). Line a baking tray with baking paper. Remove the dough from the fridge and, using a sharp knife, cut into 1.5 cm (½ in) thick discs. The biscotti will naturally squish into a nice half-moon shape as you slice through them. Place the biscotti onto the prepared baking tray.

Bake for 25 minutes or until golden around the edges. Remove them from the oven to cool.

Melt the carob and coconut oil in a small heavy-based saucepan over a low heat and stir until melted. If it goes clumpy, add a little more coconut oil and whisk with a fork.

When the biscotti are cool, dip them into the carob mixture and sprinkle with the chopped pepitas. Leave to set for 10 minutes.

Store in an airtight container. Soft biscotti will keep for 4 days; crunchy biscotti can last for more than 1 month.

Tip: Dogtella (page 167) is another great dip for the biscotti.

This is a no-bake recipe for a quick and easy muesli bar for dogs on the go.

Granola-crackle bars

Preparation time: 10 minutes
Chilling time: 40 minutes
Makes: 8–10 bars

75 g (2¾ oz) carob buttons, melted
100 g (3½ oz) coconut oil, melted
1 tablespoon peanut butter
95 g (3¼ oz/2 cups) puffed rice
55 g (2 oz/2 cups) puffed millet
55 g (2 oz/2 cups) puffed corn
1 tablespoon chia seeds
2 tablespoons pepitas (pumpkin seeds)
1 tablespoon goji berries
1 tablespoon dried blueberries

In a large bowl, combine the carob, coconut oil and peanut butter, stirring with a metal spoon. Add the remaining ingredients and stir until the carob mixture has evenly coated all the dry ingredients. You may find it easier to wear disposable gloves and use your hands to massage the dry ingredients with the carob mixture so that it coats everything well.

Line a baking tray with baking paper. Spoon the granola mixture onto the prepared baking tray, pushing down firmly with a wooden spoon or your hands to ensure it sets well. Chill in the fridge for 40 minutes or until set.

When set, carefully remove the baking paper and cut the granola into bars or squares with a large knife.

Store in an airtight container in the pantry for up to 1 month.

It's always handy to have tins (cans) of sardines in the pantry. Sardines are rich in vitamins D and B12 and in minerals, such as selenium. These lip-smacking biscuits (cookies) can have an added boost of calcium if you include the eggshells. Likewise, if you add sage, it can help soothe the digestive system.

FIONA: I've used this recipe to decorate the top of the Red velvet pupcakes (page 158) for Valentine's Day. For this, I rolled the dough to a 1 cm (½ in) thickness, used a heart-shaped cookie cutter and baked the biscuits for 10–12 minutes.

Fishy business biscuits

Preparation time: 10 minutes
Chilling time: 30 minutes
Cooking time: 25 minutes
Makes: 12 biscuits

1 garlic clove
125 g (4½ oz) tinned (canned) sardines in olive oil
2 eggs, shells optional
300 g (10½ oz/2 cups) wholemeal flour
2 tablespoons apple-cider vinegar
1 teaspoon dried sage (optional)

Preheat the oven to 190°C (375°F). Line a baking tray with baking paper.

Using a food processor with the chopping blade fitted, mince the garlic for 10 seconds. Add the tinned sardines and eggs (including the shells, if using), followed by the flour, vinegar and sage, if using. Process for 30 seconds or until it comes together to form a smooth dough.

Turn the dough out onto a floured bench and, using your hands, roll into a long sausage shape. Cover with plastic wrap and chill in the fridge for 30 minutes.

Remove the dough from the fridge and cut into 2 cm (¾ in) slices. Pinch one end of each slice slightly to make a tail shape. Alternatively, roll the dough out and use a cookie cutter. Place the biscuits on the prepared baking tray and bake for 20 minutes or until golden.

Remove from the oven and allow the biscuits to cool on a rack.

When cool, store them in an airtight container in the pantry for up to 1 week.

Tip: Make the dough, roll into a sausage shape and freeze for later.

When your puppy starts to get their second teeth they'll want to chew everything within reach. Whip up a batch of these hard bikkies (cookies) for them to nibble on instead. They won't be able to resist the glaze.

Puppy rusks

Preparation time: 15 minutes,
plus 20 minutes resting
Chilling time: 30 minutes
Cooking time: 2 hours
Makes: 15 biscuits

2 teaspoons ground sage
200 g (7 oz/2 cups) rolled oats
130 g (4½ oz/1 cup) spelt flour,
plus extra for rolling
1 egg, beaten
250 ml (8½ fl oz/1 cup) hot
water to mix

Glaze:
1 tablespoon molasses
2 tablespoons apple-cider
vinegar

Using a food processor with the chopping blade fitted, blend all the ingredients. Transfer to a bowl, cover with plastic wrap, and let the mixture rest on the bench for 20 minutes.

Line a baking tray with baking paper. On a floured surface, roll the mixture out to approximately 1.5 cm (½ in) thick and cut with a cookie cutter. Place the biscuits (cookies) on the prepared tray and chill in the fridge for 30 minutes.

To make the glaze, carefully mix together the molasses and vinegar in a small bowl.

Preheat the oven to 145°C (295°F) then bake the biscuits for 1½ hours. At this stage, remove from the oven and brush the tangy glaze over the top of each biscuit, taking care not to oversaturate the biscuits, otherwise they will be too sticky. Return to the oven and continue cooking for a further 30 minutes or until rock hard. Turn the oven off and allow the rusks to cool completely in the oven.

Remove the rusks when cool and store in an airtight container in the pantry for up to 3 months.

FIONA: *I like to make this brownie recipe in mini loaf tins so that I'll have one loaf to give away as a gift. These brownies are great treats to have at a party; they can easily be made ahead of time and frozen.*

Liver is a good source of protein and high in iron, while the blueberries are high in vitamin C and antioxidants, and the cinnamon reduces blood sugar and is great for circulation.

Blueberry and cinnamon brownie

Preparation time: 5 minutes
Cooking time: 40 minutes
Makes: 2 mini loaves

400 g (14 oz) chicken liver or lamb liver
2 eggs
150 g (5½ oz/1 cup) self-raising flour or plain (all-purpose) flour
1 teaspoon ground cinnamon, plus extra for dusting
125 ml (4 fl oz/½ cup) canola oil
1 tablespoon dried blueberries

Preheat the oven to 170°C (340°F) and line two 15 cm × 8 cm (6 in × 3¼ in) loaf tins with baking paper.

Using a food processor, purée the liver, followed by the eggs, flour, cinnamon and oil, ensuring they are well combined. Scrape down the sides with a spatula, then fold in the blueberries.

Spoon the mixture into the prepared tins and bake for 40 minutes or until a wooden skewer inserted into the centre comes out clean.

Allow the brownies to cool in the tins on a cooling rack. When cool, remove them from the tins and dust with the extra cinnamon. Cut into squares for your dog – a 50 g (1¾ oz) piece is a suitable treat size for a medium-sized dog.

Store in an airtight container in the fridge for up to 3 days or in the freezer for up to 6 weeks.

Tip: Using self-raising flour will cause the top to rise during the bake then sink slightly as the brownie cools, achieving that classic brownie look.

Serve this beautiful, light cake with some Beetroot pesto (page 84). For next-level tail wagging, use the pesto as icing and decorate with Bark (page 142) or Lamb liver treats (page 141).

Turmeric panettone

Preparation time: 10 minutes
Cooking time: 30 minutes
Makes: 6 slices

2 tablespoons turmeric
pinch of black pepper
2 eggs
125 g (4½ oz/½ cup) Greek
   yoghurt
250 g (9 oz/1⅔ cup) self-
   raising flour
2 tablespoons olive oil
2 tablespoons molasses
125 ml (4 fl oz/½ cup) oat milk
sesame seeds, for topping

Preheat the oven to 170°C (340°F). Line a 16 cm (6¼ in) round cake tin with baking paper.

Blend all the ingredients except the oat milk and sesame seeds in a food processor until combined. Scrape down the sides with a spatula, add the oat milk to let down the cake batter, then blend once more to combine.

Pour into the prepared tin and top with sesame seeds. Bake for 30 minutes or until cooked through.

Remove the panettone from the oven and transfer to a cooling rack. When cool, carefully lift the cake out of the tin.

Store in an airtight cake container for up to 3 days or cover in plastic wrap and store in the freezer for up to 6 weeks.

PETE *from* SYDNEY

Celebrations

Don't we just *love* to spoil our dogs! In this chapter, we've got the party recipes for special occasions – from pupcakes and doughnuts to cat-shaped biscuits and a snack for the humans. Be sure to take a look at our full degustation menu for your dog's party (page 169).

Celebrate your dog with this party cake. You could also use a fillet of fresh fish, such as ling or salmon, instead of tinned (canned) tuna.

Take this cake to the next level with the icing. Your party pups will be wagging their tails for second helpings for sure.

Party cake

Preparation time: 10 minutes
Cooking time: 25 minutes
Makes: 4 slices

425 g (15 oz) tinned (canned)
   tuna in olive oil
1 egg, lightly beaten
150 g (5½ oz) mashed potato
100 g (3½ oz) tinned (canned)
   red kidney beans
1 teaspoon ground fennel
1 teaspoon kelp powder
Dogtella (page 167), for icing
Bark (page 142) or Lamb
   liver treats (page 141), for
   decorating

Preheat the oven to 170°C (340°F). Line a small cake tin with baking paper. Alternatively, you can use patty pans.

Using a food processor with the chopping blade fitted, pulse all the ingredients, except the Dogtella and Bark, until combined.

Spoon into the prepared tin and bake for 25 minutes or until cooked through. If using patty pans, reduce the cooking time to 12 minutes.

Allow the cake to cool before icing with Dogtella. Decorate with either Bark or Lamb liver treats.

It's best to only ice the cake on the day you wish to serve it, otherwise the icing may crack. The un-iced cake can be kept in the fridge for up to 3 days or in the freezer, covered, for up to 1 month.

These are pretty, smell divine and are perfect for Valentine's Day. Super quick to make using a stick blender, they also freeze really well before they are iced.

Red velvet pupcakes

Preparation time: 5 minutes
Cooking time: 25 minutes
Makes: 6 pupcakes

200 g (7 oz) cooked beetroot
   (beets)
1 egg
125 ml (4 fl oz/½ cup) milk
50 ml (1¾ fl oz) olive oil
150 g (5½ oz/1 cup) plain
   (all-purpose) flour
1 teaspoon baking powder
1 teaspoon ground cinnamon
6 heart-shaped Fishy business
   biscuits (page 146)

Icing:
200 g (7 oz) cottage cheese
2 tablespoons Dogtella
   (page 167), or peanut butter

Preheat the oven to 180°C (350°F). Line a muffin tray with 6 large patty pans.

Put the beetroot, egg, milk and oil in a tall plastic mixing jug. Using a stick blender, blend on high speed for 30 seconds. Scrape down the jug with a spatula, then tip in all the dry ingredients and blend for a further 10 seconds or until combined.

Pour the mixture evenly into the patty pans and bake for 25 minutes or until cooked through.

Meanwhile, prepare the icing. Mix the ingredients in a bowl with a hand blender until combined. Chill the icing for 20 minutes to allow it to firm up slightly.

Remove the pupcakes from the oven and cool on a wire rack.

When cool, ice the pupcakes. Decorate with a little heart-shaped biscuit (cookie) to complete the Valentine feel.

It's best to only ice the pupcakes on the day you wish to serve them, otherwise the icing may crack. Un-iced pupcakes keep well in the fridge for up to 1 week or in the freezer for up to 6 weeks.

Tip: The Beetroot pesto (page 84) is another great option for icing.

This cake brings together some of our favourite recipes. There will be a few more dishes to wash up, but it is worth it.

Diwali festival cake

Preparation time: 20 minutes
Cooking time: 35 minutes
Makes: 8–10 slices

1 × Red velvet pupcakes batter
  (page 158)
1 × Turmeric panettone batter
  (page 150)
1 × Beetroot pesto (page 84),
  for icing
Bombay spice mix (page 161),
  for topping

Preheat the oven to 170°C (340°F). Line a 15 cm × 10 cm (6 in × 4 in) baking tin with baking paper.

Put each cake batter in a separate piping bag, and use a wide piping nozzle for each. Pipe the first layer of red velvet batter into the prepared tin, followed by turmeric panettone batter for the second layer. Pipe another layer of red velvet batter and a final layer of turmeric panettone batter. Bake for 35 minutes.

Allow the cake to cool before icing it with the beetroot pesto. Sprinkle the Bombay spice mix over the top.

It's best to only ice the cake on the day you wish to serve it, otherwise the icing may crack. The un-iced cake keeps well for 1 week in the fridge or stored in the freezer, covered in plastic wrap, for 1 month.

We've added this recipe to use on our Diwali festival cake. Even though you may not use all of it for the cake, trust me, you will be happy to have some leftovers. Add a little salt and chilli and you have an instant moreish aperitif accompaniment for the humans.

Bombay spice mix

Preparation time: 5 minutes
Cooking time: 5 minutes
Makes: 3 cups

1 cup puffed millet
1 cup puffed rice
1 cup fried noodles
1 tablespoon pepitas (pumpkin
    seeds)
1 teaspoon ground cinnamon
1 teaspoon ground turmeric
1 teaspoon ground fennel
1 teaspoon ground ginger
1 tablespoon cooking oil

Combine the millet, rice, noodles and pepitas in a large bowl. In a small bowl, combine all the spices. Then tip the spices over the dry ingredients and mix well.

Gently heat the oil in a large frying pan over a medium heat. Pour in the mixture and stir continuously with a wooden spoon for 5 minutes to coat evenly, taking care that it doesn't burn.

Remove from the heat and allow the mixture to cool in the frying pan before using. Store the leftovers (if any) in an airtight container. Discard the cooked spices at the bottom of the pan as they can be a little bitter.

Happy howloween! These black cats have all the scary feels on top of giving your dog's gut a boost with activated charcoal and fennel. You will need a cat-shaped cookie cutter for these special treats.

Black cats

Preparation time: 5 minutes
Chilling time: 15 minutes
Cooking time: 20 minutes
Makes: 26 cats

2 tablespoons activated
  charcoal, plus 1 tablespoon
  extra for rolling
2 teaspoons ground fennel
300 g (10½ oz/2 cups) plain
  (all-purpose) flour
2 eggs, beaten
3 tablespoons vegetable oil

Using a food processor with the chopping blade fitted, combine all the dry ingredients.

In a small bowl, combine the eggs, oil and 125 ml (4 fl oz/½ cup) water, and whisk together. Add the mixture to the food processor via the chute, with the motor running.

Once the dough appears shiny, sticky and stretchy, turn it out onto some baking paper and roll it up. Chill in the fridge for 15 minutes.

Preheat the oven to 170°C (340°F). Line a baking tray with baking paper.

Remove the dough from the fridge and unroll the baking sheet. Spread the extra charcoal over the dough to prevent it from sticking to the rolling pin. The dough will really start to behave with the extra charcoal. Roll the dough out to a thickness of 5 mm (¼ in), then use your cookie cutter to cut out your cats. Place them onto the prepared baking tray then bake them for 20 minutes.

Remove the cats from the oven and allow to cool. When cool, store in an airtight container for up to 2 weeks.

Tip: Place a sheet of baking paper on the benchtop before you start rolling your dough to avoid charcoal getting on everything.

This is technically a meal for your dog, and a healthy, festive one too. For an alternative icing, you could use the Fudge icing recipe (page 167).

Note: Neem powder is available from health food stores and Indian grocery stores.

Christmas cake

Preparation time: 10 minutes
Cooking time: 30 minutes
Makes: 4 slices

400 g (14 oz) free-range chicken thigh, bone and skin removed, then minced
90 g (3 oz) cooked barley and brown rice, cooled
60 g (2 oz) frozen mixed vegetables
55 g (2 oz) dried cranberries
85 g (3 oz) vegetable and fruit pulp (reserved from the juicer)
2 free-range eggs, whisked
handful of fresh garden herbs, finely chopped
1 teaspoon neem powder
½ teaspoon ground cinnamon
1 cucumber, sliced, for decorating
1 zucchini (courgette), sliced, for decorating

Icing:
200 g (7 oz) cottage cheese or Greek yoghurt
2 tablespoons peanut butter or Dogtella (page 167)

Preheat the oven to 200°C (400°F). Spray a 15 cm × 10 cm (6 in × 4 in) loaf tin with oil or line with baking paper.

Using a fork, combine all the ingredients except the cucumber and zucchini in a large bowl. Transfer to the prepared tin, pressing down firmly, then bake in the oven for 30 minutes or until cooked through.

Remove from the oven and allow to cool.

To make the icing, whisk the cottage cheese and peanut butter with an electric hand blender until smooth. You can store the icing in the fridge, covered, for up to 5 days.

When the cake is cool, use a palate knife or bread knife to spread the icing over the top of the cake. Decorate with slices of cucumber or zucchini, or for that extra Christmas feel, use a cookie cutter to cut the vegetables into Christmas trees.

It's best to only ice the cake on the day you wish to serve it, otherwise the icing may crack. Store any remaining cake, covered, in the fridge for up to 3 days or in the freezer for up to 1 month.

Tip: You can serve this cake raw. Just be sure to freeze it first then defrost it before serving.

Doughnut worry, we've got you covered. Jewish Hanukkah is a time when friends, family and pooches come together to rejoice. Traditionally Hanukkah foods are fried in oil, but this dog-friendly doughnut is baked.

Hanukkah doughnuts

Preparation time: 10 minutes
Cooking time: 20 minutes
Makes: 6 doughnuts

120 g (4½ oz/¾ cup) plain
    (all-purpose) flour, plus extra
    for dusting
½ teaspoon baking powder
165 g (6 oz/⅔ cup) cooked
    sweet potato, mashed and
    cold
3 tablespoons vegetable oil
2 teaspoons ground cinnamon
1 tablespoon milk (optional)
3 teaspoons sesame seeds

Preheat the oven to 170°C (340°F). Line a baking tray with baking paper.

Put the flour, baking powder, sweet potato, oil, 1 teaspoon of the cinnamon and the milk (if using) in a food processor fitted with the chopping blade and combine until it comes together like a sticky dough. Scrape down the sides with a spatula and blend for a few more seconds. You may need to add a little more flour if it is too sticky to handle.

Turn the dough out onto a floured bench. Using your hands, roll the dough into a long sausage. Cut this into 6 even slices, then roll the slices into 50 gram (1¾ oz) balls. Rest for 5 minutes, uncovered.

Bring a medium saucepan of water to the boil. Dust the end of a wooden spoon with flour, then use it to make a hole in the centre of each ball. Using a slotted spoon, carefully place each doughnut into the boiling water and simmer for 5–6 minutes.

Meanwhile, mix the remaining cinnamon and sesame seeds on a small, flat plate and set aside.

Carefully remove the doughnuts from the boiling water. While they are still wet, quickly dip them into the spiced sesame seeds, then transfer them to a lined baking tray and bake for 12–15 minutes or until cooked through.

Remove from the oven and allow them to cool on a wire rack. Store in an airtight container in the fridge for up to 3 days.

This is a dog-friendly nut spread that also works as a great icing for pupcakes. It's a fabulous way to safely share your love for peanut butter and chocolate with your dogs.

Choose xylitol-free peanut butter and never give chocolate to dogs (see page 64). Carob is not chocolate – it does not contain theobromine and is free from caffeine. Not only is carob safe for dogs, it has three times as much calcium as cocoa powder and contains a variety of healthy nutrients including magnesium, iron, potassium, protein and vitamins A, B and D.

Dogtella

Preparation time: 2 minutes in
   a blender or 15 seconds in
   a Thermomix on speed 9
Makes: 350 g (12½ oz)

200 g (7 oz) peanut butter (no
   added sugar, salt or xylitol)
100 g (3½ oz) carob powder
80 ml (2½ fl oz/⅓ cup)
   vegetable oil

Mix all the ingredients in a blender until well combined.

Store in an airtight jar in the pantry for up to 1 month.

Tip: Cashews are another nut alternative that is safe for dogs in small quantities; you can swap the peanut butter for some cashew butter. Remember, though, that nut butters are high in fat so they're best given in moderation.

Fudge icing

Preparation time: 5 minutes
Makes: 450 g (1 lb)

400 g (14 oz) of cannellini
   beans, rinsed and drained
25 g (1 oz) coconut oil, melted
1 tablespoon powdered
   dehydrated carrot (see
   page 140)
20 ml (¾ fl oz) cold water, or
   enough to give the mixture
   a fudge-like consistency

Blend all the ingredients in a food processor or Thermomix until smooth and fudge like.

If not using straight away, store in a sealed container in the fridge for up to 3 days.

The Ultimate Dawg Pawty

HAZEL *from* MELBOURNE

Wellness

Having a healthy dog is not just about what they eat; it encompasses wellness and keeping your dog's toxic load to a minimum. This chapter has a range of recipes, from bath bombs you can gift to our practical stain removal solution. All recipes are made with natural ingredients that won't harm you or your fur family.

As with food recipes, always pop a label on your finished product so you know what it is and when it was made.

Tip: Part of a dog's health includes their environment and, with that in mind, it's best to use non-toxic cleaners in your home.

PUPPY HAMPER

Know someone who has just brought a puppy home? Make a batch of Puppy rusks (page 148) and add in these essentials:

- Who farted? (Uplifting room spray, page 180)
- Stop chewing the furniture (Deterrent spray, page 180)
- Yep, accidents happen (Carpet stain removal solution, page 183)

Essential oils

Essential oils can have many healing and nurturing effects, not only on us but on our dogs too. Dogs with generalised anxiety, noise phobias or separation anxiety benefit from aromatherapy, especially lavender essential oil. It's important to only use essential oils that are 100 per cent pure and to choose essential oils that are safe for your dog.

Essential oils can be potent if used in large quantities. A dog's sense of smell, or olfaction, is much stronger than a human's; they have about 200 million olfactory receptors, which is about 40 times more than what we humans have. This means we need to be extremely careful not to add too many drops of essential oils.

A number of our wellness recipes include essential oils, but only the oils that are deemed safe for dogs. In each, we add just a few drops of each essential oil at the most.

SAFE ESSENTIAL OILS

The essential oils listed here are generally regarded as safe as per the *Essential Oils Desk Reference* published by Life Science:

- Anise
- Basil
- Bergamot
- Cardamom
- Carrot seed oil
- Chamomile (Roman)
- Citronella
- Clary sage
- Coriander
- Fennel
- Geranium
- Ginger
- Lavender
- Lemon
- Lemongrass
- Rose
- Rosemary
- Sage
- Spearmint
- Tangerine
- Tarragon
- Thyme (red)

ESSENTIAL OILS TO AVOID

Below is a list of some but not all of the common essential oils that are toxic to dogs whether ingested by mouth or topically applied to the skin:

- Citrus
- Pennyroyal
- Peppermint
- Pine
- Sweet birch
- Tea-tree
- Wintergreen
- Ylang ylang

It's great to get your dog used to having their mouth cleaned with a toothbrush from an early age. Always be gentle when brushing their gums. You could also use a soft cloth over your finger if you are game enough to put your hand in your dog's mouth.

The bicarbonate of soda (baking soda) acts as an aggregate, while the coconut oil has antifungal and antibacterial properties.

Toothpaste

Preparation time: 5 minutes
Setting time: 30 minutes
Makes: 45 ml (1½ fl oz)

2 tablespoons coconut oil, melted
2 tablespoons bicarbonate of soda (baking soda)
1 drop spearmint essential oil
1 drop aniseed essential oil
⅛ teaspoon chicken stock powder (optional)

In a small metal bowl, combine the coconut oil with the bicarbonate of soda. Add the essential oils and stir to incorporate the oils evenly into the mixture. Add the stock powder, if using, and mix through.

Tip: Remember, raw meaty bones are the best mouth and teeth cleaner.

Paws can do with some soothing, hydrating balm, not just in summer when they have to deal with hot asphalt footpaths but also in winter because ice and cold weather can be especially hard on their paws. This is a beautiful firm paw salve with healing essential oils.

Soothing paw balm

Preparation time: 20 minutes
Makes: 55 g (2 oz)

15 g (½ oz) beeswax
1 tablespoon coconut oil
20 ml (¾ fl oz) olive oil
2 drops lavender essential oil
2 drops chamomile
    essential oil
2 drops citronella essential oil

Add the beeswax, coconut oil and olive oil to a glass jar. Sit the jar in a small saucepan and fill the pan halfway with water to create a water bath. Gently simmer for 10 minutes over a low heat, stirring with a wooden skewer or chopstick until the ingredients are well combined.

Carefully remove the jar and allow the balm to cool slightly, then add the essential oils and stir to mix in.

When completely cold, cover the jar with its lid and store in a cool place. This keeps for at least 1 year.

To use, rub on your dog's paws as regularly as needed.

The healthier your dog, the stronger their immune system is at naturally repelling fleas, mites and parasites. This is a spray you can safely use on your dog's bedding and clothes. It's a combo of flea-fighting essential oils with apple-cider vinegar and neem to get on top of flea breakouts.

FIONA: Warmer weather usually brings on the fleas so be vigilant in vacuuming your carpet and washing the dog bed. I like to air Holly's blankets outside each morning and wash her blankets every 4—6 weeks. Once a week I give the blankets a liberal spray with this — it does the trick.

Note: Neem powder is available from health food stores and Indian grocery stores.

Got fleas?

Natural flea spray

Preparation time: 2—3 minutes
Makes: 250 ml (8½ fl oz)

3 drops lavender essential oil
3 drops tea-tree essential oil
3 drops eucalyptus essential oil
3 drops sage essential oil
½ teaspoon neem powder
100 ml (3½ fl oz) apple-cider vinegar

Pour the essential oils into an empty spray bottle, followed by the neem. Add 150 ml (5 fl oz) water and the apple-cider vinegar, secure the lid tightly and shake vigorously for 2 minutes to emulsify.

Allow the oils to infuse for 48 hours before using.

Tip: Cedarwood and lemongrass are good essential oils you can use to control fleas.

NEEM AND FLEAS

When dogs eat food with neem in it, fleas drop off their body. It's an ingredient in our Herbal meal supplement (page 87), Gut health smoothie (page 129) and Christmas cake (page 163) recipes.

Note: Remember that neem is only safe for dogs when it is used at the correct dosage. It can be toxic and has a bitter taste that dogs abhor.

DAISY *from* CANBERRA

Use this spray in the home or car after a big session of playtime in the park to clear out that 'wet-dog' smell or for something more sinister.

Who farted?

Uplifting room spray

Preparation time: 5 minutes
Makes: 200 ml (7 fl oz)

2 drops basil essential oil
3 drops lavender essential oil
2 drops spearmint essential oil

Carefully drop the essential oils into an empty spray bottle.

Add 200 ml (7 fl oz) water, secure the lid tightly and shake the bottle vigorously for a minute to emulsify.

Allow to infuse for 48 hours before using.

Stop chewing the furniture

Deterrent spray

Preparation time: 5 minutes
Makes: 500 ml (17 fl oz)

250 ml (8½ fl oz/1 cup) white
    vinegar
250 ml (8½ fl oz/1 cup) apple-
    cider vinegar
1 teaspoon Tabasco sauce
    (optional)

Stir all the ingredients in a glass jug until well combined. Using a funnel, transfer to an empty spray bottle. Secure the lid and shake for a minute to emulsify.

PUPPY-PROOFING YOUR HOME

Firstly, exploring and teething are all part of normal puppy development. All puppies should be safe to explore their new environment. As any previous puppy parent will attest, it is wiser to remove any item of importance from your puppy's reach before it becomes a chew toy.

Tips to avoid puppy destruction:

- Remove any electrical cords, cables and chargers.
- Keep tablecloths out of reach from curious snouts.
- Puppies like to chew shoes, carpets and furniture; use the deterrent spray (page 180) to keep them from destroying things you can't easily remove.
- If you can't watch your pup, put them in a play pen with some toys.
- Give them a good chew: old shoes, rope toys, stuffed Kongs or other non-toxic chew toys.
- Never scold your pup. Instead, use a positive interrupter (PI) – make a sound of your choosing, such as clicking your tongue – to distract your pup from the negative behaviour and follow quickly with a delicious treat (try Lamb liver treats, page 141).

It's handy to keep a couple of bottles of this in different parts of the house because accidents happen. I generally use this for removing urine stains, but it can also be used for other stains. It's always best to deal with a fresh stain straight away whenever possible.

Yep, accidents happen

Carpet stain removal solution

Preparation time: 2 minutes
Makes: 400 ml (13½ fl oz)

250 ml (8½ fl oz/1 cup) white vinegar
60 ml (2 fl oz/¼ cup) woolwash detergent
4–6 drops lavender essential oil (or safe essential oil of your choice — see page 175)

Pour the vinegar and woolwash detergent into an empty spray bottle. Add the essential oil, then top with 90 ml (3 fl oz) water. Secure the lid and shake to combine. This keeps for 1–2 years.

To remove a urine stain, clean up the area before applying the stain removal solution. If the accident has just occurred, apply paper towel to the area and remove as much of the concentrated urine. If it's been a while since the accident, move on to the next step: soak the area with tepid water several times and use an old towel or paper towel to soak up the water, applying pressure over the towel evenly with your foot to absorb the urine–water.

Give the bottle a good shake, then soak the area with the stain removal solution, carefully covering the entire area of the stain. Place another towel or paper towel over the wet area and gently apply pressure over the towel with your foot to absorb the solution.

Tip: When my dogs were puppies, I kept a couple of urine toolkits on standby. I'd have the following in my toolkit:
- *Carpet stain removal solution*
- *Disposable gloves*
- *Paper towels (and/or old towel)*

Your dog will love how they feel after a bath with these therapeutic minerals and salts.

Bath bombs

Preparation time: 10 minutes
Setting time: 30 minutes and
    a further 24 hours to cure
Makes: 12 hearts (depends on
what mould or cutter you use)

3 tablespoons coconut oil,
    melted
10 drops lavender essential oil
    (or safe essential oil of your
    choice – see page 175)
1 drop natural food colouring
    of your choice (optional)
300 g (10½ oz) bicarbonate of
    soda (baking soda)
110 g (4 oz) Epsom salts
70 g (2½ oz) oatmeal

In a medium bowl, use a metal whisk to combine the coconut oil, essential oil and food colouring (if using) with 2 tablespoons cold water, until the colour is blended evenly through the liquids.

Add the bicarbonate of soda, Epsom salts and oatmeal. The mixture will be quite stiff, requiring plenty of firm mixing with a wooden spoon for a couple of minutes. You are after a consistency of wet sand.

Spoon the mixture into your chosen moulds. Alternatively, push the bath bomb mixture firmly into a cookie cutter on a baking tray or flat surface so that it compacts. Allow to set.

The combination of these essential oils works well to alleviate symptoms of arthritis and achy joints.

Soothing massage oil

Preparation time: 5 minutes
Makes: 125 ml (4 fl oz)

125 ml (4 fl oz/½ cup)
   vegetable oil
1 drop rosemary essential oil
1 drop ginger essential oil
1 drop chamomile essential oil

Pour all the ingredients into a glass jar that has been thoroughly washed with hot, soapy water. Using a small metal whisk, or a fork, whisk together until emulsified. Seal with the lid.

Allow to infuse for 24 hours before massaging onto sore areas or joints.

Rice water is rich in vital amino acids, antioxidants, protein and vitamins B, C and E. It also contains inositol, which has been found to help restore hair affected by free radical damage from the sun and ageing.

This treatment follows the traditional Japanese yu-su-ru haircare practice and is a beautiful way to finish off your dog's bathtime. It soothes itchy skin and promotes a glossy, soft coat. For best results, apply as a post-shampoo leave-in treatment and gently massage into your dog's coat and skin before brushing it through and leaving it to dry.

Japanese rice water treatment

Preparation time: 35 minutes
Makes: 400 ml (13½ fl oz)

2 tablespoons brown rice
1 drop rosemary essential oil
1 drop citronella essential oil

First, wash the rice several times under running water to rinse out any impurities.

In a food processor, combine the washed rice with 500 ml (17 fl oz/2 cups) water. Whiz for a few seconds to break up the rice grains; the rice water will become milky. Transfer the mixture to a bowl and allow to sit for at least 30 minutes.

Using a fine sieve and a funnel, pour the rice water into a spray bottle and discard the broken rice grains. Add the essential oils and shake to emulsify.

Allow to infuse for 24 hours before using.

Tip: Plain rice water can also help with tummy upsets and diarrhoea.

Top summer tips to stay cool

1. Water! Water! Water! Next to fresh air, water is the most vital nutrient, not only for us but for our pups too, so it's particularly important to keep your dog well hydrated when the temperatures start to soar. Make sure your pup has easy access to fresh, clean drinking water. It's a good idea to have a couple of sturdy, deep bowls filled with water, just in case one gets knocked over. Water bowls can also become slimy and grimy, so make sure these are washed and wiped down every day.

2. Drop a handful of ice cubes into your dog's water bowl to keep the water cooler for longer.

3. Frozen watermelon slices, with the skin removed, and frozen blueberries are a refreshing treat that is full of antioxidants.

4. Bones given straight from the freezer are a welcome icy treat that your dog can slowly gnaw away on. Just be sure they don't demolish the bones too quickly – frozen bones can sometimes splinter. If your dog is a hoover, it's best not to give them this treat.

5. If you are feeling hot, chances are your dog is too. Bring your dog inside if it is cooler than being outside and let them rest near a fan or under the air con. Dogs love to sprawl on a cool surface, like tiles, stone or floorboards.

6. If your dog is outside when it's hot, make sure there are some shady areas where they can rest. String up a tarp so that there is always a shady spot. Keep an eye on the movement of the sun during the course of the day.

7. Avoid walking your dog in the middle of the day. Try and go for a walk early, before the sun gets too hot, or in the cooler part of the evening after the sun goes down. If you are out for a long walk, remember to take a water bottle, and a collapsible water bowl, so you can all stay hydrated.

8. Remember if the ground burns your feet, it means it's burning their paws, too. Paws can easily get burnt; soothe dry, cracked paws with a paw balm (see page 177).

9. Have a dip! A shallow paddling pool is great for your dog to cool off in; you can always add a tablespoon of magnesium salts for added healing benefits for their joints.

10. Make cooling down a game. Some dogs thoroughly enjoy being squirted with the hose to cool off.

11. NEVER leave your dog in the car in warmer weather, especially with the windows closed. And never tie them up outside in the middle of the day.

12. Get groomed. Make sure your dog's grooming is up to scratch and get rid of all that untidy fur so that they will stay cool. Even brushing away matted hair keeps the air flow cooler for your pup.

Fun fact: Did you know that your dog's fur remains flat when it's hot and fluffs up when it's cold? Their fur assists with thermoregulation.

Fireworks

Fireworks can be extremely troubling for our furry friends. While we can't protect our dogs from hearing them entirely, we can make their experience a little less frightening. When it comes to noise desensitisation, there is no such thing as starting too soon. Start preparing weeks (ideally, months) in advance to give your dog plenty of time to get chill.

<u>JACQUI</u>: I found these training tips worked well for Radar. Don't get me wrong, he still does not like fireworks, but instead of racing around, barking hysterically like we're under attack, he now sits in his bed and protests with an occasional bark and a manageable amount of grumbling.

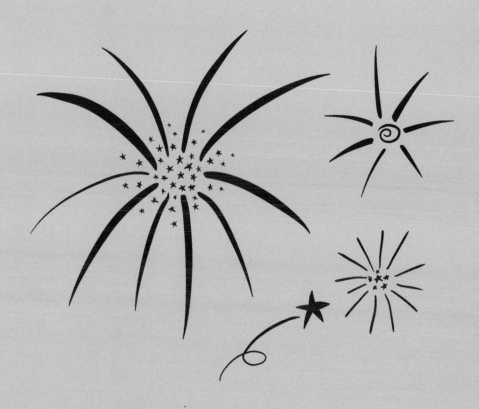

STEP 1

Search online for audio clips of fireworks. The idea is to play the audio clips in a controlled way to help desensitise your dog. Start low and slow. Play the audio clips for around 10 minutes, two to three times per day – that will be plenty. And start at a volume you can barely hear – you can build up gradually.

STEP 2

While playing the audio clips, give your dog something positive to focus on. Play with them, and try not to act differently or draw attention to the sound. The goal is to keep your dog settled and calm.

STEP 3

Only increase the volume if your dog is happy and relaxed and is not stimulated by the sound.

STEP 4

Repeat playing the audio until your dog no longer reacts to the sounds, even when you turn the volume up.

FINALLY

When you know that fireworks are likely, prepare a comfy, quiet area for your dog, and include some of their favourite toys. Wherever possible, you want your dog to associate the noise with something positive. To reduce the impact of sudden fireworks, keep the radio or television on. Remain calm and act normal. Dogs are very perceptive, so if they sense you're worried, then that might cause them to feel anxious too. Good luck!

> *Tip: If you find that thunderstorms freak out your pup, then you can try the same approach with audio clips of thunder.*

Doga

FIONA: I'm not talking about getting your pup to do headstands or the plough pose. However, doing yoga with your pup, or doga, has a multitude of benefits for their wellbeing as well as yours. Dogs know when you are stressed, so doing yoga is beneficial for both of you. Yoga is about being in the moment and dogs love being in union with their pack.

Doga stretches and relaxes us and our dogs, and also strengthens your bond with your fur baby. Dogs are naturally drawn to yoga and many people can attest to how much their dog loves to participate in their yoga practice. In doga, humans help dogs perform doga poses and humans perform yoga poses while their dogs mill around. This practice is purely a mindfulness exercise; try it out and see how Zen your dog becomes. Holly just sleeps by my side or else lies on her back wanting a belly rub.

HEALTH BENEFITS OF DOGA

This mindfulness-based exercise encourages positive outcomes:

- For the humans, doing yoga can help reduce blood pressure, improve posture, increase vitality, aid relaxation and relieve anxiety and stress.
- Your dog will benefit from touch; massage can help their circulation.
- Doga provides one-on-one time: the eye contact and full attention you give your dog during this time helps teach trust and strengthens the bond you share.
- Doga is a fun practice that can also be a great socialising experience for dogs.

EASY DOGA POSE

This is a doga practice that only takes between 3–5 minutes (or longer, if you wish). Remember never to force your dog into a pose.

Begin in a relaxed Cobbler's pose. Sit on the ground comfortably with your dog in between your legs. Keep the soles of your feet together with your legs bent, your knees down and relaxed, your back straight and your shoulders pulled back.

Start stroking your dog, moving from the head and working your way out to the rest of their body. Rub their ears (they have acupressure points). Gently rub their jaw. Move on to massaging their front legs, shoulders, then move along their spine to their hind legs. You can also massage gently over their stomach. While you do this, stretch forward over them to give your back a nice stretch.

Pawmaste!

Index

Acknowledgements

FIONA

Ahhh, that sigh of completion and appreciation at the end of a beautiful, heartfelt project.

I have so many good people to acknowledge and thank. First of all, a special big thank you goes to the amazing Jane Willson, our publisher – I adore Jane's straight talking, her right-on-the-money speak, not to mention her enthusiasm for the project and ongoing encouragement; to Joanna Wong, we could not have asked for a better project editor, so Zen, and with an incredible eye for detail, putting everything together so pawfectly; to Marg Bowman, for her wonderful copyediting; to Melanie Faith Dove, for her beautiful work and expert dog wrangling; to Alex Robertson and Barb Newton for their generous assistance on shoot days; and to the talented Andy Warren, with his beautiful design concept. Thank you, Hardie Grant – such an amazing team to work with.

A big hug and kiss to my supportive, loving husband, Andrew, the yang to my yin. Love everything we do together, and he really does believe my dog eats better than me (him!); and to my two beautiful, creative sons, Alex and Charles, who always encourage my creative doggie madness, ideas and pursuits. To my mother, who has always cooked everything from scratch and encouraged me to cook healthy food from scratch.

A heartfelt thanks to my PAWDinkum community. A special thanks to Dr Andrew Trezise for his encouragement and support for PAWDinkum.

A big thank you to the talented Jacqui Melville. I look forward to our next catch up in person to raise a glass for all our hard work on this beautiful project. If it wasn't for COVID-19, we would have seen this project out together.

JACQUI

To my chief taste tester and happy sidekick, Radar. Thank you for being the best dog our family could hope to have!

Thank you to Jane Wilson, Joanna Wong, Marg Bowman and the wonderful team at Hardie Grant. To Andy Warren for the fantastic design and to Melanie Faith Dove for stepping in when COVID-19 prevented me from travelling to Melbourne for the shoot. You have done a gorgeous job, thank you!

To my posse of supreme supporters who encouraged me to step out of my lane and try something new. To my hairy pack of Chiswick taste testers and their owners, whose friendships I value so much – thank you!

Thank you to Tracey for planting the seed, my mum for her unwavering support, and to my awesome husband, Chris, without whose belief in me this project would never have moved from idea to published book.

And last but certainly not least, a huge thank you and a big high five to my co-author and collaborator Fiona Rigg, for her unwavering dedication and unending enthusiasm for this project and all things doggie.